Your Horse's Mind

Your Horse's Mind

Léonie Marshall

The Crowood Press

First published in 1996 by
The Crowood Press Ltd
Ramsbury, Marlborough
Wiltshire SN8 2HR

www.crowood.com

Paperback edition 2003

British Library Cataloguing-in-Publication Data
A catalogue record for this book is available from the British Library.

ISBN 1 86126 566 2

Picture Credits
All photographs by Vanessa Britton
Line drawings by Rona Knowles

Typeset by Phoenix Typesetting, Burley-in-Wharfedale, West Yorkshire

Printed and bound in Great Britain by Bookcraft, Midsomer Norton

CONTENTS

Introduction

In humans, psychology is the scientific study of the functions of the mind and of how the mind affects behaviour in a given context. Although much research has been done on the way the horse thinks, with reasons given as to why he acts as he does, this information is necessarily limited because the horse cannot speak. Most conclusions therefore are drawn from observation and experience.

The object of this book is to help owners to analyse the reasons why their horses think as they do; and also to assess how much their actions are responsible for the way a horse behaves. Anticipating how a horse will react given a particular set of circumstances only comes from experience, as each one can react so differently.

Although the horse's mental characteristics may be generalized there are always exceptions, besides which there are some differences in these characteristics between breeds within the species; a native pony, for example, will react differently to a Thoroughbred, and an Arabian will differ to a Shire. However, most of its responses are dictated by two main criteria: first, it is governed by its inherent instincts, behavioural characteristics instilled over the centuries in the course of natural evolution; second it behaves in response to Man's demands. For this reason, the book can be divided into two main parts: the horse's contribution to the partnership (Chapters 1–6), and Man's contribution (Chapters 7–13). Both factors can give rise to problems although I personally have found that the higher proportion has always occurred from the second. This is largely because Man fails to comprehend the horse's mind.

In order to appreciate this more fully it is necessary to understand the biological basis of psychology, founded in hereditary influences. Genetics is the study of the inheritance of behavioural and physical characteristics such as ability and temperament, height, bone structure, hair and eye colour. All characteristics are dependent on heredity and environment.

Man's perception of his horse's learning capacity and its ability to develop should come from an understanding of its history and of its inborn fears; he must also realize that much of its capability comes from a highly retentive memory. The potential of each individual animal can only be realized by providing it with a suitable environment and by giving it experiences that it can comprehend.

I have found during many years of teaching people and training horses that the first priority is for Man to accept his failings and to be prepared to learn. The horse is a remarkable animal that can, if properly understood, be taught and controlled, and made to perform astonishing feats in the company of its master or mistress. Above all it needs to feel secure both in the stable and out of it, and this should be one of the chief aims of every owner.

This book will endeavour to explain how the horse's mind reacts to certain stimuli, and how these elicit behavioural responses that may or may not be what we expect.

PART ONE

CHAPTER 1

Instinctive Behaviour

To understand the horse's mind fully and to appreciate why he reacts to us as he does, we need to know something of his history because so many of his actions have to do with deep-rooted instincts.

Millions of years ago the earliest known relative of the horse was little bigger than a medium-sized dog, and he spent his time foraging under shrubberies and in long undergrowth. During that time the earth was mainly swamp and marsh and this little creature possessed toes on his feet, not hooves, because this made it easier for him to move about; hooves would have caused him to sink into the mire. At the time *Eohippus*, as he was known, had four true toes and a 'splint' for a fifth on his forefeet, and three toes with one or two 'splints' on his hind feet. These splints indicate that in an even earlier time there were probably horse-like creatures with five toes.

Fossils and remains discovered over the centuries have revealed conclusively how the horse evolved into what he is today.

The physical changes experienced by *Eohippus* were due to climatic alterations affecting the planet Earth: it became cooler, and as it did so it became drier with the result that wet marsh areas turned into wide, drier tracts of land. This change also influenced the vegetation, which instead of being largely leaves and foliage and undergrowth began to evolve as grass and prairie. As this took place *Eohippus* was increasingly obliged to use his eyes and nose to detect his enemies, relying on speed to escape them; thus he gradually became taller and faster as the years passed, changing from a slow browsing animal to a quick grazing one.

The term 'the survival of the fittest' was especially appropriate during this period, and only those who adapted to the changes in the environment managed to survive. Development of smell, sight and hearing was of great importance. In the survivors, the nostrils became bigger and more sensitive; the eyes, instead of being placed frontally on the head, were positioned

Eohippus *was little bigger than a medium-size doe, evolving over millions of years into the horse we know today.*

more and more to the side to give a better range of vision; and the ears which had been small and insignificant grew in size and mobility. The horse could now 'sense' his adversary as well or better than any other animal.

He also developed the advantage of great speed. As the earth altered, so did his feet. Gone were the spreading toes necessary to cope with wet, marshy ground: now he possessed compact hooves ideal for galloping across the hard surface of the plains in order to outrun his predators. He had in fact become a power machine with a highly sensitive and well developed sense of self-preservation.

The Herd Animal

The present-day horse has evolved from these origins; to understand him even further we need to study his behaviour in his natural environment, where first and foremost he runs in a herd or group.

Any group or herd of horses requires a leader, and in natural circumstances a stallion will fill this role, responding to instinctive sexual motives which will drive him to keep and control the rest of the herd as he wants. Some stallions like to keep their mares in a tight group, and become quite annoyed if one should stray. In the wild this would be sensible from the point of view of protection, because one animal on its own would be extremely vulnerable.

Dominance results partly from temperament and partly from sexual libido. We used to breed Shetlands, and at one time had an exceedingly dominant stallion who would instantly round up any

If several horses are turned out together they will instinctively gather into a group.

mare that appeared too independent; he would also frequently circle his grazing mares and foals and drive them into a huddle so that he could then move them on to the part of the field *he* wanted them to graze. By contrast we had another stallion who was much more relaxed; when put out with the same mares he allowed them much more freedom and seemed quite happy to let them 'do their own thing'. The stallions were quite different, the first older and more aggressive by nature, the second younger and rather mild in temperament.

However, even the more placid stallion was still clearly in control. Only once did one of the mares dispute his leadership.

She was old and crotchety, and had once been almost starved to death so if there was any food about she generally made a point of laying claim to it. The other mares knew to keep their distance, having already been kicked, but one day she and the stallion had a terrific set-to which

In the wild there would be only one stallion to each group of mares; should a stallion from another group challenge or try to encroach they would fight to the death unless one gave way. The young male foals in the herd would be driven away as they reached puberty; they would then form their own groups.

surprisingly went on for some time – although it rather proved, I thought, how courageous mares can be when defending their rights, and how they probably do fight to the death in certain circumstances. But stallions do not give way either, and this one continued to show fight until the old mare gave in.

In our herd, the only time that either stallion allowed a mare to leave the group was when she was about to foal. She would choose a suitable place under a hedge on a flat piece of ground, probably so the foal would not roll away from her, and give birth while the stallion stood guard. He stood nearby, not interfering at all but remaining calmly alert. After a few hours the mare and the newly suckling foal would join the herd.

The younger stallion was a good deal smaller than most of the mares so he had some difficulty in mounting them for covering, but the way he overcame this problem was interesting: he would chivvy the mare he wished to serve into a down-hill position so that he was on the higher ground, and then he had no trouble at all! Horses may not be able to reason, but they do often show a great deal of instinctive good sense.

My intention in giving these examples is to show that horses do follow a pre-determined pattern of behaviour that has been passed down over many hundreds of years, and that when we take them away from that environment we must allow for adjustment.

Natural Weaning and Orphans

A mare and very young foal will be quickly taken back into the group – other wild

> Because pregnancy normally occurs regularly every year, mares may become quite run down unless their 'keep' is good, as so much of their energy and condition is devoted to nourishing their foal.

animals having disposed of the afterbirth – and they will run together until weaning time. In the natural state a mare will wean her own yearling foal by kicking it or chasing it away as she approaches foaling again; often this may be only a short time beforehand, unless her milk has dried up earlier.

> The maternal instinct is very strong, and a mare's sense of protection can get her into trouble with other mares, especially if she has lost her own foal.

If in the wild a mare dies giving birth, her foal would also die and be disposed of by other animals. If, however, she dies at a later date, the young animal may be 'adopted' by one of the other mares, though this is not so usual. In domesticity an orphan foal can be brought up on the bottle, and inevitably it will look to its human foster parent in the same way that it would have to its own mother. An orphan we had at one time appeared to be happier in human company than with its own species, and it had to be 'weaned' in a similar way.

Because of her inborn desire to protect her young, a mare will naturally become very upset when in a domestic situation the time comes for her foal to be taken

In the wild, a mare and her new-born foal are quickly incorporated back into the herd.

away. This has to happen, however, in order that the mare can resume a normal life, and so the foal can be introduced to the social structure which will control its future life. In order to minimize the anxiety inevitably experienced by both dam and foal, they should be separated and taken well out of hearing range of each other; after a few hours of calling they will generally settle down.

Calling

The horse's main form of communication one to another is whinnying, and this may vary from the gentle whicker of a mother to its foal, to the loud screeching of one horse shouting to its friend. Vocal contact is essential to the animal in the wild, firstly because should it become separated from the group whinnying will help it to find its way back. Whinnying may also be a warning of impending danger. In the stallion's case it draws attention to him, reminding the group that he is in charge. At mating time a pair will call to each other, reinforcing their desire.

In a domesticated situation the horse will display these primitive reflexes, and in certain situations they will erupt quite spontaneously.

Signals

Horses use many signals to talk to each other, some of which as humans we understand while others are more obscure. One of the methods they use which can be aggravating to their owners is to prance and snort, and anything which they consider alarming or exciting could incite this reaction. For example at a show recently one of the youngsters in the in-hand class fell over, and this instantly caused a furore of snorting as the alarm message was passed round the ring. Once the animal was on its feet, however, the others settled down and the problem was over. Then in a neighbouring ring one of the foals got loose causing consternation from its mother, and her whinnying recall was soon copied by the other mares in the class as they hastened to ensure the safety of their own foals.

Boundaries and Protection

There are, of course, no imposed boundaries in the wild, but a stallion will impose his own by urinating, passing faeces and rolling, all of which will be familiar to his own group and the smell of which will warn off others not within the group. When necessary he will move his group to other areas in search of food, and will then establish a new boundary.

Although his primary task is to mate with his mares he will be very aware of the need to protect them and their foals. Any animals of any species may pose a threat but even when they do not, such as sheep or cattle, the stallion may still chase them off, or at least not allow them close to the herd. It is quite common to see a stallion chase a dog or even a human if he considers they might take liberties.

Natural Defences

In a domestic situation there is obviously no likelihood of a predator dropping out of a tree onto the horse's back, but in the course of his evolution this is exactly what did happen – or he was chased to an unfortunate end! Flight would be his first instinctive response, together with bucking, kicking, rearing and biting following closely afterwards. This is what we have to contend with when we try to teach the horse to accept our relatively unusual demands.

Coping with Seasonal Weather

Animals living in the wild will react instinctively against excessive sun, rain, wind, snow and so on. Horses will stand with their backs to driving rain, or they will shelter from hot sun under the trees. Mares will protect their foals by standing on the 'weather' side, and a stallion may round up his group during excessively bad conditions.

Variable external temperatures also cause a fluctuation in the growth of each animal's coat. In winter it is of course thick and may be long, gradually reducing to quite a thin covering by summer.

Natural oils and dirt will protect the animal from the worst weather, and he will roll repeatedly to ensure that he is protected.

As the length and thickness of his coat are governed by changes of temperature, so he is able to anticipate the changing seasons – and with this the need perhaps to travel to more suitable areas. All these factors also govern the mating season, which begins in the spring and can continue until autumn.

The Sexual Urge

A stallion's sexual urges will be stimulated by the mare's secretions and he will 'cover' her as soon as she is ready and willing to stand for him. Ovulation can occur at very different times during the season, and there are no rules as to when a mare will be ready. A good vet will be able to tell by internal examination, if required; otherwise at a stud the mare will be 'teased' to see if she will stand. Some mares are less keen than others, but generally it is unnecessary and unwise to allow a stallion to mate with a mare when she obviously objects to his attentions. She will allow him to do his job on the right day.

Death

In a herd situation natural wastage is inevitable, and those members within the

The stallion has been led to the mare to see if she is ready to be covered but she kicks out so it is probably too early. In the wild the stallion will 'test' his mares daily and cover those who 'stand' for him.

This mare shows she is ready for the stallion by emitting secretion and 'standing' for him.

group accept it calmly. Even a mare which has lost her foal seems to accept that it has died, and will get on with day-to-day living. In domesticity, one horse left on its own may appear to be pining for its friend and indeed this may be so; but it is not because it misses friendship as we know it, but rather because it is disliking its solitary state. Horses essentially prefer companions.

If the horse left behind is able to see for itself that its friend is indeed dead, it will in my experience, accept the fact; whereas if one were simply taken away, the horse left behind would call for it for some time.

Self-Preservation

One of the strongest of all the inherited urges is that of self-preservation: the horse will look after himself first, and he will only suppress this predominant instinct in obedience to our demands if he is confident that he can trust us totally. Such trust is not easily acquired, and we have to earn it over many months and years. Even when we do have it, if the horse finds himself in a potentially threatening situation, he may well revert and follow his natural instincts. Indeed sometimes we may be heartily thankful to him for getting us out of a nasty predicament, especially when jumping; and in all honesty it is rather nice to know that because he wants to save himself, if we do not interfere, he will look after us also!

Because of this strong inclination horses are continuously aware of possible dangers, and almost seem to look for them on occasions. As a result, certain types spend their whole time spooking or shying at what seem to us to be imaginary objects. To the horse, however, these objects must be real, and whatever they are they send off alarm signals which cause it to take flight. Trying to reassure a frightened horse can be very difficult and only by gradually building up trust can its nervousness be overcome.

The absolute necessity for food and water may lead horses into trouble. My New Forest pony had learned to fend for herself before she was brought into a

> Horses kept in fields and in groups are far closer to their natural environment than those which are confined in stables. They respond to deep, in-born inclinations and will use their ingenuity to survive. For example, in a really harsh winter animals will obtain liquid by licking snow, and will sometimes use a forefoot to break the ice in a water trough.

domestic situation, and she never forgot her 'rules of survival'. Thus whenever the quality of the 'keep' in her paddock began to deteriorate, she would get out and go in search of better. One day she almost met her Waterloo actually swimming across a lake to reach a field of rich grass on the other side!

Owners should be aware that the natural reaction to fear is flight.

Domesticity

It is believed that horses were first used by man for draught purposes long before they were ridden (before this they were reared and kept for food), and as such they were of great benefit to those working the land. Later they came to be considered as a means of ridden transport, and in particular were much used by warring tribesmen. However, as regards domesticity, because of their evolutionary pattern horses have always found it difficult to adapt to a restricted environment, and many of their behavioural problems stem from this fact.

Man's Response

When we shut a horse up and tell him to behave we deprive him of his natural methods of self-help; he is then effectively at a loss, and may well react in ways we do not expect. He should therefore be given all the help he needs, from being correctly

The combined problems of first, providing foodstuffs that suit a horse's physical needs, and second, of harnessing his natural energies, have troubled Man for centuries. Given the right circumstances, horses become willing partners with Man; misunderstood, however, they can be quite the opposite.

fed to being routinely exercised. Left to himself a horse will graze most of the time, a régime which suits his digestive system; he will be constantly walking about and may have a good gallop round each day too – foals in particular will do this. This behavioural pattern is of optimum natural benefit to the various systems which constitute his metabolism. When we shut him in a stable we deprive him of these options, so in order to keep him happy and well we should help him to adapt, using our knowledge of his instinctive requirements.

CHAPTER 2

The Senses

The Sense of Smell

The sense of smell is the most primitive of the senses; it is determined by chemical substances known as pheromones that are secreted in the skin and are released for the purpose of detection by another animal of the same species. This being understood, let us consider in what way the horse's sense of smell aids him in thought and action.

Identifying Objects

We may ask, does the horse think before he smells an object, or does he smell it and then think about it; and what does he do when he has thought about it? There is clearly some mental process going on continuously or there would be no action at all – but this is often mere curiosity. It is not until the horse has smelt the object he is curious about that he draws a conclusion as to its safety, or whether it should be viewed with suspicion; and his reaction will be either calm acceptance or an instinctive desire to flee. If his decision is the latter, left to his own devices he will avoid that object forever after; only if *we* take a hand in the matter will he be persuaded otherwise.

So what is the sort of object that frightens a horse, and why? It is my experience that any object not previously assessed by smell is considered potentially dangerous, and investigation is therefore necessary to make this assessment. The horse may do this by first of all trying to make a decision from a safe distance, and then drawing nearer to finalize the matter. Any object that has a potent odour, or one that is unnatural to the horse, such as a creosoted stable or a human wearing perfume, can set off alarm signals. He may conclude that something he finds unpleasant is best avoided; on the other hand if it seems harmless he may accept it without fuss.

Most of those who ride will have experienced being unable to pass some object they meet, the horse snorting in horror and refusing to go forwards. This may be due to something he has smelt. It is a well known fact that horses are fearful of both the smell of blood and of pigs and have to

---

Concerning the smell of blood, I can well remember having difficulty getting one of my horses up a woodland path. Eventually I got near enough to discover the corpse of a dead rabbit, newly killed. I had to dismount and dispose of it before I could go any further! On another occasion I was riding quietly along a lane when in an instant my horse swung round and tried to gallop off. I only discovered much later that there was a pig farm further down the road!

---

be helped to overcome these fears. One can well imagine why they might be frightened of blood, but a dislike of pigs is not so clear; perhaps at one time in evolution the pig was an enemy of the horse! Buying a pig or two may not be a practical proposition, but most horses get over this sort of phobia if exposed to it for long enough.

All the evidence points to the fact that horses have a more highly developed sense of smell than humans.

The Importance of Experience

As well as objects that may require a good sniff in order to test their safety, there are many other occasions when the sense of smell causes alarm to a horse. These are associated with any new experience or circumstance in which the horse finds himself. It will generally be to do with a change in environment, a change of food, an unusual atmosphere and so on. Even changing from one field to another or to the next-door stable can be worrying to the horse, and until he has had a good sniff about he will not be satisfied.

Identification through Smell

Being able to identify through smell is vital to the horse. Once he has been introduced to an object or experience and has identified it he may no longer be worried about it; but he also needs to identify certain factors within his own species.

The very first of these is being able to distinguish his mother. In a group situation this may be quite difficult for the young foal who has only just arrived into the world, and at this point he will rely on his mother to know the smell of her own young. Gradually the foal will learn her smell too and they will form a bond.

Identification by smell is essential to determine sex, age or possible animosity.

In a domestic situation when a mare is separated from the others it is more obvious to the foal who his mother is, although bonding does not always take place at once. From the smell of colostrum, and usually aided by his mother, the foal will learn to suckle. The smell of his faeces may be one aspect of her recognition for him, as also are the pheromones or smell messages that are produced by the skin glands and communicated by contact.

Horses that live in a 'group' situation will identify each other's sex by sniffing; and age is also apparently assessed in this manner, as most older horses will be more tolerant towards a foal or a youngster than they would be towards a horse of their own age which might be a threat. Moreover as horses get older they certainly use their sense of smell to distinguish between friend and foe. The expressive action known as 'flehmen' – raising the upper lip

This expressive act of raising the upper lip is known as 'flehmen', and is associated with a strong or unusual smell.

after smelling something – is often used after an initial greeting. It is also used by stallions during courtship and sometimes when a horse has smelt something strong or unusual.

Communication

The initial reaction of one horse to another is a direct result of the kind of smell that each gives out. In a familiar group hierarchy the scent of each individual will already be known and therefore not a worry. But as far as a horse is concerned,

A reaction that often occurs when two or more horses greet each other is to squeal or to strike out with a forefoot. This can be very painful if you are in the line of fire, so you should be prepared for it to happen; we therefore suggest that allowing horses to greet each other by sniffing either when being held, or when ridden, is rather an unwise practice.

A greeting between two horses often involves 'striking out', a form of play to them, but painful to us if caught in the line of fire.

it is essential that he discovers whether a stranger is friendly or of sexual interest, and he will wish to smell him or her all over in order to determine this fact.

Most horses are gregarious by nature and like to be together; therefore after a preliminary skirmish the vibrations given off are generally friendly. Once a horse has decided to accept another as his friend, smelling usually stops unless they live separately, in which case when they do meet they may smell each other again to confirm the relationship.

Establishing and Assessing Territory

Horses rely on their sense of smell to define their territories. This can be seen when turning a horse out into a strange field, as he will generally gallop round it, going up to each boundary fence to see what it is made of as well as whether it will limit his activities.

Many, especially stallions, will urinate to define their area, and they and others will smell the urine or faeces already present. By doing this they assess the association with their own species, and can establish that a mare is present if the excreta is recent.

Water is located more by smell than by sight. Often it takes quite a time to find, and may only be discovered after quite a lot of sniffing around. It may be, however, that food is of greater interest to the horse and that he makes that assessment before setting out to find a water supply.

The Sense of Smell to Discern Food

I think it would be safe to assume that a horse's sense of smell takes precedence over his sense of taste when inspecting foodstuffs, as often having smelled something he will not touch it. Most horse carers will undoubtedly have experienced the disappointment of having bought a horse some wonderfully smelling new food (or so it appears to us), only to find that he rejects it. Often his suspicion is merely because it is new, and once he has tried it he will eat it; but if the smell is in any way unpleasant to him he may never be persuaded. This is especially true in the case of most forms of veterinary powders when mixed with a short feed. In the days of worming powders the horse would very often refuse to touch the food in which the powder was mixed, regardless of how many succulent carrots or apples were added to it! In fact if he caught even a whiff of it he would apparently starve rather than eat it!

Man's Response

It is important to appreciate that the horse has to use his sense of smell to distinguish between friend and foe or what seems to him to be good or bad, and that this method of identification inevitably makes him wary. Knowing this, we should respond to his dilemma with common sense and sensitivity; we should understand the extent to which he feels threatened, and should make allowance by being patient.

Most horses view any stranger with suspicion, because they must assess humans in the same way that they assess members of their own species. In particular this applies to anyone with a slightly unusual smell such as the veterinary surgeon or the farrier. Normally though, once these individuals are accepted they are treated with calm – unless they behave in a way that causes the horse pain. The horse's sense of smell quickly becomes discerning, and in this sort of instance those individuals may cause the horse to display much consternation the minute he recalls the scent of either. Similarly he will instantly recognize humans whom he has learned to like or dislike. Horses can also identify such events as the female monthly cycle; this in particular may affect a stallion's behaviour.

The Sense of Hearing

The range and acuteness of a horse's hearing is largely unknown. Most of us have no doubt experienced our horse apparently hearing something when we ourselves do not, so we may assume that he picks up signals before us. This may depend on the frequency or density (intensity or loudness) of the signal.

Because a horse's ears can rotate, they can pick up the maximum amount of sound. All messages received by the ears are transmitted by nerves connected to the brain; this, however, can only analyse one message at a time, so as the sounds – which are quite different in pitch and tone – arrive, the ensuing analysis sometimes becomes confused, resulting in unexpected responses. So even though we know the horse has heard the same sound that we have, it may not be identified in his mind. Also we are bombarded by so many

Pricking of the ears is the most obvious sign that the horse has heard something, but he can hear equally well by rotating his ears.

Initial hearing of a sound may need to be further identified by sight, in which case the horse will want to turn his head, not simply move his ears.

sounds all the time that it is unlikely we would remember whether our horse had heard any one particular sound before or not; in which case the analysis is even more complicated.

To gain maximum hearing effect, horses point their ears in the direction of the sound which alerts them, generally brought to them by wind-born stimulus. From early on in their lives they learn to distinguish and identify sounds as friendly, threatening, soothing or scolding; thus the soft whicker of a mare to her foal is clearly in a different category to the raucous squeal of one horse threatening another. The tone of the message received is therefore important, so that a softly praising human voice will be related to a safe and pleasant experience whereas a sharper, loud noise would indicate something alarming and potentially dangerous.

In the course of training a horse will 'tune in' to the voice of his trainer and quickly learns to distinguish different words of command by their tone, even from the moment they are first used (see Chapter 4). The ears will be seen constantly flicking to and fro to pick up these signals.

As already discussed in Chapter 1 an important method of communication between horses is the whinny, its intensity and message varying enormously depending on the mental state of the horse at the time. Thus it is used as a warning of impending danger; to recall an inquisitive foal; as a greeting; as a signal to a human; as a sign of nervousness or insecurity; as a cry for help. Horses will also snort, a method of expression used mainly to alert another or to convey extreme excitement; in the latter case it may incite others to join in, an invitation to gallop about together making things all the more fun.

Interpreting a Horse's Reactions

The horse relies largely on his hearing to determine enemy from friend, and depending on the way in which the sound waves are analysed by his brain, he will react accordingly. Thus if a sound is familiar we may be able to anticipate his reactions: for instance, if you know that your horse has been frightened by a truck in the past, you will know what his reaction is likely to be. Whereas the clank of a bucket at feed-time means pleasure, and you will be aware of this. Sometimes the horse will respond unexpectedly, for example a leaf falling out of the hedge into the road may cause him to shy. A harmless leaf you say to yourself, feeling annoyed; he has seen millions of leaves in his life. But maybe this is a time to pause for thought and to reflect on the message that was relayed, because as far as the horse is concerned, anything falling or appearing unexpectedly can pose a threat and his instinctive answer to it is to flee.

Man's Response

We should consider ourselves to be the guardians of our horses' minds. We may shoulder this responsibility well or badly, but even if we don't like the idea, it is our duty nevertheless to try and understand the way our horses think. So whatever *we* may think the horse had heard, we will only know by his reaction to it, and it is up to us to teach and to reassure him by using the voice to help him gain confidence. The human voice is one of the most effective training aids.

The Sense of Touch

If we are to understand why touching is important we first need to realize the actual physical need of the horse in his original state.

Touch to Establish Status

For the horse, recognition and identification is achieved by contact during which pheromones (skin messages) can be passed from one horse to another. In the wild, the horse will rely on these messages to inform him whether he is greeting one of his own species or more particularly a member of his own group or herd.

We have all seen how horses make contact with each other. An initial greeting is often accompanied by much exuberance, but it is essentially a test of supremacy because whatever the sex of the animal, a pecking order has to be established. After a certain amount of skirmishing one protagonist will normally submit to the other, possibly the younger because a younger animal will nearly always concede to the older. Of course there will always be those who dispute leadership and this may result in more serious argument; in their wild state one party will eventually give way, although it may incur considerable injury in the process. In a domestic situation, however, we are responsible for keeping order, and should therefore control such confrontations. A one-to-one meeting is clearly easier to resolve.

Horses chewing at each other's withers is a sign of friendship and is a simple act of touching.

After an initial meeting some horses appear to become particular friends and will constantly touch each other in apparent affection, often biting each other's withers. They are also probably passing messages, either of a sexual nature or because one is dominant and is making that point clear. Wither scratching evidently gives much mutual satisfaction, but of all the time spent touching each other, probably more relates to the establishing of dominance, particularly when one animal is asserting him- or herself as head of the family. Size or sex seem to matter very little in this instance; we once had a Shetland mare who was always in charge no matter how big her companions, and she established this position in no uncertain terms by biting or kicking anyone who stepped out of line!

Touch to Identify Objects

As we know ourselves, a great deal can be assessed through touch. We can quickly establish whether an object is hot or cold, soft or hard, or whether it is pleasant or painful. We analyse the messages our body receives from the contact we make. In his natural state a horse will draw his own conclusions as to the safety or other-wise of a particular object; but when he is under our control it is our responsibility to be very tactful in introducing anything new to him, and to be very aware of his physical sensitivity.

We do know that the skin of some animals is more sensitive than that of others, and that skin sensitivity also varies according to its position on the body; horses in particular have areas that are more sensitive than others, for example around the nostrils and mouth which are well supplied with whiskers and sensory cells. Sensitivity not only depends on the thickness of the coat or skin, but also on the number of receptors at different points of the skin. Knowing where these receptors are may not be essential to the everyday horseman, but it is important to be aware that the cells of the nervous system only become sensitive when sufficiently stimulated, as in the giving of an effective aid (see Chapter 4).

The pain threshold of many horses is apparently quite high, as is evident by the lack of response by some to coercion, but the thinner the skin the more sensitive it tends to be as, for example, in most Thoroughbreds. However, this cannot automatically be assumed to be the case, as all types of horse can be insensitive: thus some don't mind being brushed with a stiff dandy brush at all, while others hate it; and some react immediately to a mere flick from the whip, whereas others need a good sharp slap.

Flinching from the feel of some object may mean that the horse has simply not experienced it before, but he may also be telling us that it hurts. A horse's reaction to the feel of a particular object will send a signal, and it is our responsibility to try and interpret it accurately, according to the individual horse.

Touch to Establish Security

As mentioned in the introduction, feeling secure is of prime importance to the horse, and in this respect a good deal of reassurance can be given once a relationship is established by a friendly pat or stroke on the neck. Right from the start a mother will reassure her offspring and make it feel protected by nuzzling or licking it, and this fundamental act is ingrained into its

One of the best ways to reassure or reward the horse is to stroke or pat him on the neck.

mind. As owners we can in some way replace this natural form of giving comfort by the simple act of a pat.

Horses will also touch each other to establish a feeling of security, sending messages through physical contact to dispel doubts and give mutual confidence. We had one particular horse which when placed in the line-up at a show would determinedly lean on his neighbour; as long as he could maintain this contact he remained perfectly calm, but if it was lost he became quite hysterical. I have since come across this behavioural trait more than once in horses of a nervous disposition or those which have repeatedly changed home.

Man's Response

The horse therefore needs to be made to feel secure by the way we handle him, and we do not always react in a way which makes him feel secure. We often misinterpret his motives, although he seldom misinterprets ours. One reason for this is that we humans unwittingly give off certain signals which betray our emotional state. For example, when experiencing emotional tension we may blush or sweat; the heart beats faster; the mouth becomes dry and the muscles tense. The horse is sensitive to these signals, receiving them as electrical impulses transmitted automatically but unconsciously by our bodies; so in a way he knows more about us at that moment than we do ourselves!

The Sense of Sight

The size and position of the eyes is such that the horse has a wide range of sight, although his peripheral vision is not as acute as his central vision; thus he may be startled by normally familiar objects if they occur on the edge of his visual field because he cannot see them clearly. The same objects seen in the centre of his visual field would cause no untoward response.

Because the horse has a narrow binocular field of vision it is common sense to point his head in the direction in which you want to go, especially when riding him (this would seem obvious, but is frequently not done, see Chapter 4). It is particularly important if the horse is blind in one eye – and I have known several – and needs to have his range of vision organized for him by his rider. In all cases of impaired vision or actual blindness of an eye I have found that there is no particular limit to the work that the horse can do; although I imagine a horse required to gallop at high speed could find this a major handicap.

Perception

From an early age horses learn to rely on sight: to look for their mothers or friends, to locate food or water and to watch out for predators or any other object of potential danger, including humans. With regard to this latter fact, even when the horse is older he may flee in the opposite direction at the sight of an approaching human.

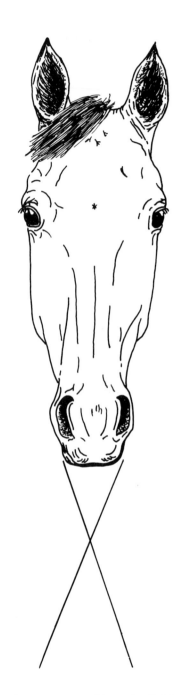

Horses have a narrow binocular field of vision which is why it helps to point the head in the direction he is to go.

There could be many reasons for this: he may not wish to be caught due to some unpleasant experience, or perhaps he is spooked by some garment that flaps about, or maybe he simply does not want his freedom disturbed. Clothes, umbrellas, shopping bags, even bales of hay can cause great suspicion until properly identified, and this sometimes takes quite a long time as his eye adjusts to the different shapes and colours.

The question of whether horses see in colour still seems unproven. Many believe that horses do see colours, at least in a limited range; others maintain that all they see are varying degrees of light and dark. Whatever is the real answer I think we all know from experience that horses do distinguish differences, even though this may only be while the eye is changing focus. Anyone who has had to jump a fence from bright sunlight into a dark wood, or who has ridden in the spotlight at Wembley, will know that this often causes a horse to spook; as do varying shades of colour on a jump pole.

On the other hand shapes and patterns are, I think, quite distinct to the horse: thus he will walk over a rustic pole quite happily, but if you paint white blobs on it he is likely to shy away in fright. This applies also to sunlight and shadow on the ground; thus a sudden patch of light may make him jump, or he may be persuaded to skip over a line of shadow created by a branch. Similarly I well remember our horse's horror when shark's teeth became a big feature in show jumping, and the trouble caused by a chessboard wall. However, once he had had the chance to assess these sights properly the horse accepted then with equanimity.

At night when there are no such patterns or alterations of light the horse has good vision, and can be relied on to see where he is going better than we can.

Visual Signals

There are many signs that horses give to each other that convey information, telling of another's sex or age, liking or dislike. A mare will display her readiness to be covered by 'showing' to the stallion (lifting her tail and presenting her rear end), and he responds by becoming more animated and sexually aroused. Young foals show their submission to an older horse by 'snapping' (opening and shutting the mouth). Older horses may show impatience or dislike by putting their ears back, snapping their teeth together, curling their lips, swishing their tail, or actively kicking or biting. Liking may be expressed by approaching with ears pricked in a calm, non-threatening manner.

Man's Response

Being aware of how the horse sees should enable us to introduce him to new objects in such a way that he will not be frightened or worried. Horses have long memories and will never forget something they have seen in the past that has been unpleasant in some way.

Sometimes they may seem to be imagining something that isn't there: they may shy or refuse to go near an object, and although initially their fear may be genuine, it may lead to stubborn disobedience. If dealt with perceptively in the first instance, however, it can be overcome before it develops into a phobia.

The Sense of Taste

It is generally thought that if left to himself a horse will choose appropriate, non-poisonous foodstuffs, and will find for himself any minerals deficient in his habitat. In general I subscribe to this theory; to quote an example, I once knew of a native pony which lived most of its life in a paddock with a yew tree (known to be quite deadly), and died of old age at twenty-six! On the other hand, we also once had in our care a pony that became thinner and thinner, and eventually had to be put down. The post mortem revealed acute ragwort poisoning. The interesting thing was that the pony had lived with several others in the same field, none of which were affected, so the assumption was that they had not eaten the weed. The suggestion made by the vet was that the pony which had eaten it had done so because it found scraping a living from well eaten pasture too much of a struggle; or that possibly it had come to like the taste. Presumably in the wild the herd moves on when food becomes scarce and so there is little need to resort to weeds and suchlike; but in a restricted environment anything may be better than nothing. It is therefore vital that in such circumstances suitable feed is provided.

This example indicates that the taste receptors sometimes fail to determine suitable foodstuffs. Taste receptors are groups of chemically sensitive cells found

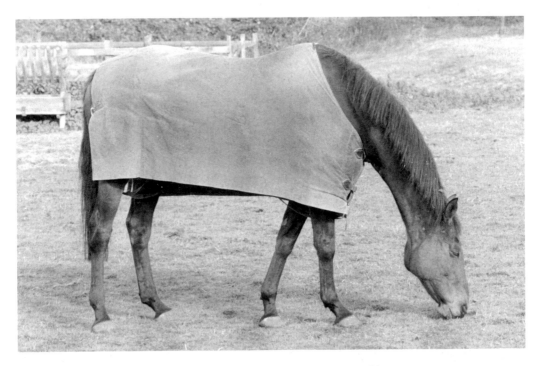

Horses grazing on well-worn pastures may be tempted to eat something unsuitable which they would not do in the wild, as the herd would simply move on.

on the horse's tongue and commonly called taste buds; they are also found in other parts of the mouth and at the back of the throat. Scientifically it is known that horses respond to salts and acids and can tolerate tastes that would be far too bitter to humans. They can also pick up sweet and sour tastes, but we do not know how sensitive they are to them.

In his natural state the horse would exist on a variety of plain herbage or leaves, so it is not surprising that when faced with quite different types of foodstuffs he can be suspicious to the point of not eating. Although his taste receptors may inform him that a certain foodstuff is suitable if he will just give it a try, there is still no guarantee that he will follow it through; besides, there seems to be a great variation in taste preferences.

Horses in a domestic environment can often choose what they eat, as owners frequently provide a variety; if one particular foodstuff is rejected they will provide something else. In general I would say that I have found horses to be discerning as regards quality, especially with hay which presumably gives an unpleasant sour taste if it has not been made well. Dusty oats, stale sugar beet or mildewed nuts would normally be left, while anything fresh is gobbled up. Oats have always been a favourite among the horses I have owned, as have carrots and apples,

When veterinary preparations have to be mixed in with a feed they should be disguised if the horse is not to be put off.

so I presume that the taste of these is especially acceptable.

Some horses will take sugar if it is offered straightaway, while others will not touch it; sometimes it is an acquired taste. On the other hand I have found that very few horses refuse mints; they actually seem to enjoy keeping them in their mouths to suck. There are certain other tastes that are obviously disliked; one of these is creosote which I have used to good effect in deterring rug-tearers or horses that crib-bite or windsuck.

Horses can easily be put off their food. I remember having trouble because a veterinary preparation I had been given had to be mixed into the feed; the horse would start to eat but would then decide he did not like it. I tried to persuade him by adding various titbits and mixing the feed thoroughly – but to no avail. If I removed the feed and placed another minus the medicine in the manger the horse would still not touch it. I could only imagine that the taste lingered in the manger, and in fact it was not until it was scrubbed clean that he would take food from it again. Of course the horse's sense of smell would undoubtedly have played a part in this.

Man's Response

The aim should be to provide suitable foodstuffs which an individual horse will eat because he likes the taste. Common sense should be used when introducing a new substance – and also ingenuity, when a fussy horse must be tempted to eat by finding something he really likes.

CHAPTER 3

Temperament

Temperament may be described as an individual's distinct nature and character. It is inherited, but the way it develops is the result of the experiences the horse may have, and our handling of it.

There are certain ingredients that are likely to make the horse behave as he does. For instance, a highly strung horse is more likely to develop stable vices or to be fractious during its training, while one that is laid-back may well produce idle or even stubborn tendencies.

Many disobediences and vices that erupt during a horse's lifetime are attributed to 'his temperament', but are in fact due to bad training or because we have failed to understand why he has behaved in a particular way. If we can accept that each horse is an individual with its own distinct nature and mental characteristics, then we are more likely not to generalize, but to seek to learn about that particular animal.

Breeding for Temperament

As far as breeding horses or ponies for riding is concerned, much thought goes into the choice of parents in order not only to achieve good specimens of the species but also ones with as straightforward and willing a temperament as possible. The best method of producing a suitable temperament is by selective breeding, where two animals with similar traits are matched to each other; the resulting offspring can be judged on the basis of performance, which will also depend on its level of intelligence.

Out-crossing is practised to introduce particular qualities, although some breeders prefer to line breed in order to sustain qualities that they already have.

A prepotent stallion will pass on worthwhile qualities such as good bone and conformation, good temperament and so on, and when an equable nature is a prerequisite, the best option is clearly to mate two animals of calm disposition, or at least animals with no particular quirks. Unfortunately this equation does not always work out, as those horses which have the best temperaments may be very poor specimens in build, and those with good conformation may not have the temperament. And although owners may be tempted to use an animal with good conformation but a dubious temperament, this is an unwise practice.

'Line breeding' is the mating of animals related within a line, or to a common ancestor. This differs from in-breeding when closely related relatives are mated continually, regardless of traits in each which when combined result in a doubling-up of the weakest genetic links.

When selecting a stallion it is useful to look into his background and if possible to see his progeny, because this will give the prospective breeder an opportunity to investigate which of his characteristics have been passed on. The ability of a stallion to 'stamp' his stock is very important, especially in the matter of temperament. It is also a good idea to observe older stock if and when they compete in order to determine their reactions under competition conditions. However, nothing is ever certain, even though our intentions may be good and however carefully we plan a breeding programme. Thus even if the chosen parents seem compatible, it may become apparent that some not-so-suitable genes from a more distant relative have been inherited by our youngsters. Nevertheless we are obliged to cope with the result of the union.

stud owned two stallions which were complete opposites as regards temperament: one was very highly strung, the other was almost idle by nature, and during the time I was there the progeny from each was quite distinct and easy to recognize. The highly strung one produced tense foals that rushed about worrying themselves and getting into trouble, while the foals of the other one were all thoroughly laid back and completely calm.

Mares can also imbue their foals with certain foibles of temperament. For example, a mare that dislikes humans for some reason may cause her foal to take the same attitude; this is especially easy to see in relation to catching. Thus mares which do not want to be caught invariably gallop about, causing the foal to join in too; whereas the ones who like being caught and petted stand quietly with their foals beside them.

Inherited Temperament

Temperament is evident even in young foals, and they will soon display the traits of their beautiful but cranky father or the calm nature of their mother or vice-versa. Some will prove stroppy even at an early age, while others will let you do anything with them right from the start. Of course they may just be copying their mother's reactions to situations, which in a way masks their own natural inclinations, and it may be hard to separate this tendency from the foal's own personality; but as its own nature develops it inevitably comes to the fore.

The differences in temperament inherent in young foals sired by different stallions are often quite obvious, as I found while living on an Arab stud. The

Handling Foals

The foal born into a domestic environment is immediately exposed to human contact, and from this moment on his inherited temperament will be shaped and will develop for better or worse. The way in which a handler asserts his authority will definitively affect the young animal's view of life and so it is of the utmost importance that everything he does is done with forethought and with adequate knowledge. The youngster must nevertheless learn to comply with his handler's wishes rather than follow his natural reactions, a lesson which some accept more willingly than others.

How submissive a foal really is becomes apparent the first time he is asked to do something he does not wish to do, such as

As early as possible in his life the foal should be introduced to new things. This one has already happily accepted a rug.

being led away from his mother, and it is in such a situation that his temperament is likely to show its true colours. Thus he may show that he is by nature unwilling, by taking a stubborn or aggressive attitude; under pressure he may, even at that age, try to kick in resentment, and will put his ears back in a threatening manner. On the other hand, foals which are happy to accept discipline at this age are likely to be co-operative and easy to handle throughout their training. Highly strung foals will become increasingly nervous or agitated as rules are imposed upon them.

The way in which a foal accepts these rules of behaviour is therefore tremendously varied, but will certainly be an indication of his regard, or otherwise, for his trainer. However, although discipline should always be enforced both for reasons of safety and because it will hold good for the horse's entire future, it should be done sensibly. There is no point in creating a larger problem than you started with because of an insensitive approach. As regards restraint, it is never easy to assess how much is ideal: too much and it causes inhibitions; too little and it may not achieve the required result. The fact that it must be done is undeniable, however, and even at this early stage it is important that the young animal should be taught what is right and what is wrong as the instigation of these good manners influence the rest of his life.

Thus if a foal threatens to, or succeeds in nipping, a sharp slap by the hand round his nose should teach him not to do it. If he kicks, a good smack on the offending leg or across his flank will inform him that this is not allowed. Most foals will accept these corrections quite happily, although the odd one will answer back; in this circumstance the punishment should be reinforced so that the youngster does not get away with any sort of disobedience. But it is as well to remember that, just like humans, horses also go through rebellious stages in their development, when they seek to test their strength and to see what power they may gain.

The horse's individual temperament should be taken into account throughout his life because it may affect so many aspects of it. And if we fail to appreciate the effect his nature is bound to have on his behaviour, the horse may end up being categorized as a 'temperamental swine' whereas with more understanding he would have been a useful animal.

Problems of Temperament Caused by Man

Although the horse's temperament is inherited from his parents and will basically remain unaltered throughout his life, it can appear to change as a result of certain experiences.

Rehabilitating the Racehorse

Racehorses have a particularly difficult time when, for whatever reason, they come out of racing and are expected to follow some other discipline. The Thoroughbred was primarily intended for racing because of his build, speed and stamina. He is well suited to this purpose, and because galloping with others is an inborn characteristic he is happy doing that job. Many difficulties may arise, however, if he is removed from this environment. First of all keeping the horse on its own may be a problem, and expecting it to work alone, too, since during the whole of its early life it will have been used to living in a yard full of horses and going out in a string. This is entirely different to the 'one-man, one-horse' set-up it now finds itself in. Secondly, the racehorse will not have been taught conventional 'aids' as understood and used by the average horse owner and it will need re-educating which will take time.

Another major problem is that the horse will almost certainly be prevented from behaving as he has been used to, and he will find this very confusing. Restraint to a Thoroughbred can be very irksome as generally it has an instinctive desire to go fast, and when prevented becomes anxious. And it is important to appreciate that anxiety in the horse can cause him to behave in such a way that he gives the impression of being in opposition to his rider. If the rider doesn't know how to deal

> Many ex-racehorses find slow work hard to accept mentally and also difficult to carry out physically, largely because they will have developed a certain musculature so that a change in work can be, literally, painful. It is rather like being fit to run a marathon and then being asked to do ballroom dancing!

with the horse's anxiety, or doesn't understand the reasons behind it, or deals with it unsympathetically, he will have problems.

The same can be said of the way the owner handles this type of horse in the stable. Moreover in a racing yard the daily routine will be entirely different to that in the 'one-horse' owner's yard, and this in itself can make the horse feel insecure and frightened. Any fear or worry can cause fretfulness, loss of condition or the development of stable vices (see Chapter 7). Thus by putting the horse into a situation where he does not feel comfortable we are asking for trouble unless we are prepared to make concessions and allowances.

Many racehorses do adapt well to other spheres and become stars in their field, but there are many instances when their resistance to change is blamed on their temperament, and this is unfair and shortsighted.

Recognizing Physical Limitations

Both temperament and physical ability vary from one breed to another, and so it is impossible to judge whether a horse's resistance or dislike of what he is being asked to do is due to his temperament, or to his physical limitations.

For instance, the Highland pony is bred to carry heavy loads across difficult terrain, work which requires him to go slowly and steadily. Taken out of that environment, it is clear that whatever training he has, he will never be suitable for galloping fast or becoming a great athlete! And although many Highland ponies and others have become excellent performers in a variety of fields, it is important always to appreciate their origins and not to expect too much. It is very easy to accuse an animal of being lazy and uncooperative when the inherent nature of his breed type in fact predisposes him to behave in this way.

Physical limitations must be taken into account with animals of any age, particularly the very young and the very old, as nothing is more unfair than to accuse them of having a bad temperament when it is their physical capacity which prevents them from doing what you want. For instance I know one very old racehorse whose owner declares him to have a temperament problem, objecting that he constantly fights with his rider and clearly resents the work he is being asked to do. However, this is not really surprising considering that he is old, stiff and arthritic!

Problems Arising When Breaking In

Many things can go wrong at this stage of the horse's life, problems that can affect his whole outlook. For example, we were once sent a pony to break in which already had a reputation for having a dubious temperament, and it did indeed prove to be exceedingly difficult, especially when a saddle was produced. And it was only some while afterwards that the owner admitted that it had been saddled before, but had broken loose and galloped off with the saddle banging about round its back legs!

There have been many other times when bad behaviour has been blamed on the temperament of the animal, instead of on the shortcomings of the owner. For example, we knew a nine-year-old mare who seemed unreasonably terrified if her

Carelessness when riding or breaking horses causes fear and subsequent problems. Flapping stirrups or reins being trodden on are two common occurrences.

rider slipped up her neck; her owner/rider, however, was convinced she was being downright awkward. But when we looked into her past history, we discovered she had been broken late in life, and that the conclusion to her first experience of someone riding her had been the rider falling off and clutching her round her head!

Unusual Problems

Very often it is some bad experience, all but obscured in the past, that makes a horse behave oddly, and which takes some rooting out when attempting to explain and thus remedy such behaviour. There may be a physical reason too: for example, there was the case of a horse with a reputation for being very nappy, although his nappiness took on a rather unusual form. Thus when he was in company he would follow another horse absolutely anywhere, but if alongside or in front he would not go at all! Of course there are many horses which when ridden will not take the lead,

Horses of all ages can be temperamental in the sense that they display a degree of opposition to the wishes of their owner or rider. But we must always be sympathetic to the individual, and try to find out why he is behaving in this way. Young animals must be taught what to do, and older ones should be given the benefit of the doubt.

but this one wouldn't even go into the stable unless another went in before him. His owner was distracted by his apparent total stubbornness – until eventually it was discovered that the poor horse was nearly blind!

Some horses behave very badly as a direct result of the environment in which they have been kept. For example horses raised in ranch style conditions have to be rounded up for operations such as branding and castration, and so their only experience of humans is related to pain; it is not surprising, therefore, that these animals look upon us as the enemy, and as a defence try to avoid ever being touched. We had two such horses which had been imported and were bought at a sale. If we had not known about their past we would certainly have categorized them as having bad temperaments, since they both bit and kicked with great determination!

A sale can be a very traumatic experience for a horse, and if one has been 'round the sales' for some reason he may be genuinely in a very nervous state; he may express his worries in all manner of ways and will need time to learn what his new owner wants of him. With sympathetic handling, however, he should get over any fears.

There are many stories or myths about horses of certain colours being good or bad in their temperament and therefore easy or difficult to train. I am bound to say that my experience has been that no colour has proved to be more awkward than another. One of the most willing and equable of animals I ever had was a chestnut mare and one of the most unpleasant was a bay gelding. Over the years we have owned horses of every possible colour and type and a black thoroughbred was as easy to handle as a black cob, chestnuts, browns, greys, coloureds, spotted – none was more difficult than the other. Of course, we have had problems of temperament and occasionally nasty horses, but I can think of no particular colour that has been worse than another.

I think it is a pity that a particular colour should brand a horse as possibly having a tricky personality. I have found that almost all horses function in a similar way and that it is man's lack of understanding that brings out the bad in them.

Characteristics of Different Breeds

There is little doubt that the different breeds have their own distinctive characteristics, which to a certain extent dictate temperament.

The Thoroughbred

The Thoroughbred is a good example. Many are highly strung, being at times over-sensitive and difficult to handle as a result, and a great deal of tact is needed if such animals are to reach their potential. Many of them cannot take concerted pres-

Thoroughbreds can have sensitive temperaments, and because they have been bred to race they sometimes find other work difficult to accept.

sure when ridden, for example, but need more time and patience than other, more slow-witted horses. And if a rider uses force they may become almost hysterical or even actively resistant. New experiences often cause them anxiety, but if these are dealt with calmly the situation will not get out of hand. Sometimes, because of their volatile temperament, these animals are categorized by humans as stupid or crazy – but this is unfair, and is mainly because we have misinterpreted the reasons for their behaving in such a way; if there had been better understanding of their fears and worries some awkward situations could have been avoided.

Take the case of the young Thoroughbred being taken for a hack for the first time on his own. To begin with he is worried at leaving his familiar surroundings and any friends who may be left behind, so he is reluctant to leave the yard. Also he does not yet fully understand his rider's aids.

He therefore resists, and tries to turn round to go back home. His rider hits him. He is dismayed. Because he feels threatened both by fear of the unknown and by aids that he does not fully understand, he reacts by throwing himself about in an effort to get back to the place he knows: his familiar stable yard. He may rear up and unbalance himself, skidding on the slippery road. His rider, however, believes him to be a nasty brute, perhaps even accuses him of being a brainless creature. Either way the horse's future is bleak, and he has already become a possible hazard both to himself and his rider.

Of course a knowledgeable rider will have anticipated the whole situation and will have prevented it from occurring by riding out in company with an older horse as 'nanny'.

My point is that it is so easy for the rider to put the horse in a position where he cannot help himself and then to blame him for the outcome.

Warmbloods and Cross-Bred Horses

Warmbloods and horses of mixed breeding such as the Irish Draught crosses are generally of a moderate disposition. Their temperament is such that they can take pressures that others cannot, and they are not easily flustered. They can be frustrating to teach as some are slow to learn, but once a lesson is fully retained it is there for good.

The Native Breeds

Each native breed has its own distinctive

The warmblood is generally temperamentally suited to most forms of competitive work. It has been bred to have the build and action that many people want.

characteristics, and these vary considerably between breeds. Many of the smaller types such as the Shetland, the Dartmoor and the Exmoor have a reputation for being lazy, although in my experience any laziness is chiefly because they are allowed to be – and some I have to say are the complete opposite! Children are not strong riders and consequently ponies often get away with things that they wouldn't with an adult; and getting out of work would certainly be one of them! They will always do their own thing if they can: their independence is notorious!

The Welsh breeds seem to be inherently lively, from the diminutive section A to the powerful section D ponies; in fact they can be somewhat sharp, with very quick reactions which will often catch us humans unawares! They are intelligent and have quick minds, and this can be used to great advantage.

The Arab

Over the years Arabs have had the indignity of being categorized as somewhat cranky. Their nature is certainly outgoing and they are independent, but the ones I have had to train have been no different as regards temperament to any other horse. All horses are individuals and should be treated accordingly.

Temperament in the Sexes

Stallions

There are many myths about horses of a different sex having this or that temperament. Of course it is true that a stallion will show certain temperamental tendencies which may make him awkward to deal with occasionally, but this is more to do with his sexual drive than his basic *temperament*, and there are just as many laid back stallions as there are lively ones. It is the control imposed on them that makes them well behaved, though if allowed to develop in the wrong way their different individual temperaments will lead them to react differently to discipline. For instance, a stallion with a laid back nature will probably accept his punishment meekly when corrected, while a more volatile character might react aggressively. Those that are aggressive must nevertheless be taught to toe the line by firm handling or they will get out of hand.

To cope with a stallion's temperament the owner must know how to be firm; if it senses any sign of weakness the horse will take control. Stallions are essentially dominant and very strong, alert and intelligent, and they do require an owner who understands how to exert control, but without constantly nagging. Many stallions *become* bad tempered because they are constantly hit for biting or barging. However, this sort of behaviour is an integral part of their sexual drive, and it does not mean that they necessarily have a bad temperament. Of course they should accept correction like any other horse, but it should be done in the right way. One good clout is worth many small ones!

> Many of the best horses in the world are stallions, and this is true in all spheres of competition. They are normally full of vitality and power which if channelled properly can be a great asset.

Mares

Mares may also have a common ingredient of temperament in that they are often wilful, and determined to have their own way. The age-old maternal instinct I believe plays a part in this, and it will sometimes override a mare's true temperament. Otherwise there is very little difference, their tough outlook being a distinct asset if used correctly.

The character of some mares is affected when they are in season, and they can be more difficult to deal with at that time. Their reaction varies: some will be more lethargic, others will be fractious; and some show actual resentment to their work. There are also mares who seem to be completely unaffected by being in season. I have found that a naturally willing mare generally remains willing even during her season, while a less willing ones becomes duller.

Some mares will kick out if they are ridden when they are in season, and this habit is sometimes considered to be a problem of temperament; but it is often due to trouble with the ovaries, and has nothing whatever to do with a resistance to her actual work. A vet should be called in to deal with the matter.

Geldings

Geldings are reputed to have mainly easy temperaments, since they are never subject to the sexual urges which might compromise trainability. This I have found to be an advantage in some ways and a disadvantage in others. They may be easier to train, but they have of course lost the natural exuberance of the entire which, when it works in your favour, outshines the rest.

Rigs

A rig is a male animal which has had an unsatisfactory castration and is left with some libido; it can be a nuisance to own as it is not sure exactly how to behave. Usually there is no problem with the owner, the difficulties arising in the rig's relationship to other animals. It is quite likely to chase mares or other geldings round a field, and may go through the 'mounting' process. The rig itself is frustrated and may be bad-tempered, and it can cause a great deal of annoyance to others.

We owned one particular pony which, if let out in a field with a mare in season, would chase her round until she was exhausted and in a white lather. This sort of behaviour is, of course, distressing for both animals concerned.

Displays of Temperament

I believe it is a reasonable practice to allow young animals the freedom to show their true temperament so as to find out the best way to channel each individual. As long as any display of temperament is done in a controlled environment it can be useful. Thus it is interesting to see how a horse reacts when he is turned loose by himself or with others. Does he go roaring round the field behaving like a lunatic, or does he go out calmly and graze? Of course other factors must be considered such as whether he has been cooped up in a stable up to this point, or if he is desperate for grass; but even so, his natural temperament will almost certainly show through.

Observing the reaction of one horse to another is also useful, as it tells us whether he is sociable, or aggressive, or

> Older horses who have 'been around' may not show their temperamental preferences so clearly, and it may take some time before we get to know them sufficiently well to understand their problems.

passive, and so on. He will let us know from his behaviour what sort of 'person' he is.

Health and Management

An important factor which undoubtedly affects a horse's temperament is the environment in which the animal is asked to live. Some methods of keeping horses are very restrictive (see Chapter 7) and to my mind wholly unacceptable, and can give rise to many problems. It is vital to appreciate that a horse which is not happy in his mind is not going to be happy in his work, and to this end it is an owner's responsibility to provide suitable housing and exercise areas, and to care for the horse's general health.

As regards health, the horse is a very long-suffering animal in many respects, but he cannot tell us when he doesn't feel up to work, and we won't necessarily realize unless he is actually lame or obviously ill. He will certainly give us signals indicating that he doesn't feel well (see Chapter 8), and we must learn to read these if we are to get the best out of him.

Horses cannot reason that if they are lame or ill they will get out of work, although sometimes we believe that they do! So from the signals that the horse gives us we should accept that his malady is not 'put on', but that he is genuinely using the only methods at his disposal to convey his distress.

To work when in pain makes *us* disagreeable, and the horse is no different. He will be reluctant to do what you want when he is ridden, and may try to avoid obeying you by overt resistance.

Man's Response

All horses have problems relating to temperament but as already mentioned, many of these are man-made. Thus some horses undoubtedly suffer when separated from others, and some hate being stabled. Some are neurotic about other animals, or develop stable vices as a reaction to an excessively restricted lifestyle. But behavioural problems come from régimes that *we* impose upon the horse – and then we blame his temperament!

Certain problems *are* to do with temperament: nervous horses that fret and will not eat, for example; or the slothful type who stand about getting fat on air! However, in general I believe that it is the responsibility of every owner to find out how his own horse 'ticks', and to treat him accordingly.

CHAPTER 4

The Horse's Learning Capacity

Learning is the mental process of perception and memory that provides the horse with the necessary knowledge to give appropriate responses.

The Learning Mechanism

From the moment he is born the horse starts to learn. He begins by finding his mother's teats and then learning to suck. He automatically uses his limbs, but he has to learn how to control them. Some of his learning is instinctive, inherited from decades of evolution; the rest is discovered or taught. His process of learning evolves from curiosity and a powerful memory.

He uses his senses to evaluate, and from their messages will come his response. First, however, a stimulus must be provided, and this stimulus then becomes associated with a certain response with which it was not previously associated. This may have occurred by accident, or it may have been the answer to the question which the person providing the stimulus asked for. Either way, if the horse is rewarded for his correct answer he will store the knowledge in his brain to be used when the question is asked again.

Responses come in two forms: unplanned, and planned. In the case of the unplanned or unlearnt response – such as shying because an object moves unexpectedly for example – it would be possible to change this to a planned response by apparently rewarding the horse every time he shied at something unexpected: the pat we give him simply to reassure him *he* may in fact interpret as a reward for something he should do. Clearly we must teach him to differentiate, but it does serve to demonstrate how horses can learn something incorrect by a false move on our part.

Method of Learning

In a wild state the horse learns the limits of social behaviour from other members of his group who use biting or kicking, their main means of correction, for this purpose. In association with Man the horse has to learn his place from our treatment of him. Thus if we are too soft he will get the wrong impression and believe that he can do as he likes, like a spoilt child. If we are too severe his spirit will be cowed and he may become sullen and uncooperative. A balance must therefore be found so that he knows exactly where he stands: if he does as he is asked he will be rewarded, if he bullies or is nasty he will be punished.

As with the group system in the wild

In the wild, horses establish their own pecking order and this process involves the use of teeth and hooves. When the position is horse versus human, the owner must be prepared to assert himself.

where pain is inflicted by the use of the teeth or hooves, so in a domestic situation the way to learn is through various forms of discomfort or pain, followed by a reward. Horses accept this system perfectly happily if it is applied properly, and they will never hold it against us once a rapport has been established.

Establishing a Rapport

As horses are physically so much stronger than we are it is necessary for us to use our ingenuity and common sense when dealing with them. It would be foolish to put oneself in a position of vulnerability and risk an accident, so even from his earliest days as a foal the horse should be in no doubt that you are his friend but also his master. This can entail some harsh lessons if he misbehaves. Also he must learn that when he wishes to show you his

dislike for something, even though the perhaps violent way he behaves will be entirely natural to him, he will not be allowed to develop in such a way.

The use of the whip will be inevitable when teaching the horse to make the right responses. Remember, too, that his hide is tough and is covered by hair, so it will need more than a faint-hearted tap to make an impression. The important factor from the horse's point of view is that he knows *why* he is being corrected or punished; once this is properly established in his mind he rarely abuses it.

Building up a rapport on the ground is the first essential. Once a foal reaches

> Horses love praise, and there is no doubt they respond if we make our appreciation clear to them.

It is interesting to consider whether a horse's age has any relevance to his capacity to learn. In my experience it has virtually no relevance, and I have found that horses of any age learn perfectly adequately. This is truly remarkable when I consider how difficult I find it to retain newly learned knowledge now, in my later years! Also, it is amazing how older horses can re-learn and completely alter their way of going. Of course, the older the animal the harder it is for him to change physically, and he may also have some problem that prevents alteration; but this aside, he is at least mentally able.

Young animals probably do have the advantage, as long as their owners have the necessary knowledge to teach them correctly in the first place. Because their minds are untutored they do need a gradual process of training, but because their brains are uncluttered, progress can be made quite fast.

learns he often discovers by mistake, but if these lead to some experience that suits him, they will be stored in the mind, remembered, and acted upon again at a later date.

This amazing power therefore should be used to its maximum effect by teaching the horse those things that we want him to do. As has been proved by 'planned' responses, if enough repetition is involved this reinforces the thought in the memory bank to such an extent that it will never be forgotten. The following example should illustrate this:

If a horse is taken into a field and asked to canter, but off no particular 'aids', he will choose the leg he wishes to lead with, which will be the one most comfortable for him. And if left to his own devices the whole time, he will almost certainly learn to favour that lead to the point where he will never use the other one. But should the same horse be asked to canter off specific aids telling him which leg to lead with, and if he obeys and is rewarded for doing so, he will subsequently answer correctly.

Repeating an exercise also assists the horse's physical development, thus making it easier for him to give the right responses. Because this is so, mentally he will also be happy and this will make him even more willing to please.

weaning he will have become fairly independent of his mother, but at that moment of separation he will look to us for security. And if this is given in the right way he will become a willing partner. Thus whatever we wish to do after this initial bonding, the relationship between man and horse should be considered a partnership; so when we decide upon our ambitions we must also judge in what way the horse is likely to respond to them.

The Power of Memory

All the horse's learning is based on his power of memory (it is fairly certain that a horse cannot rationalize). The things he

If a horse is tired from lack of fitness his mind will be as unreceptive as his body. In order to build up strength and muscle the horse's training should be regular and systematic. He needs to practise on a daily basis rather like a ballet dancer or gymnast if he is to make progress.

Control through Communication

Basically we control the horse from the ground, or from the saddle or when driving. We control the horse on the ground chiefly by use of the voice and the whip.

The Voice as an Aid

The human voice is invaluable in achieving a good result and should be used from the very beginning to aid understanding. It can be used in so many ways, changing in tone and strength, and combined with a soothing stroke or pat on the neck will soon teach the horse what is wanted. And by praising the horse for his achievements we should quickly gain his cooperation.

It is important to decide exactly what words you wish to use and how you want them to sound. In fact the actual words themselves seem to be irrelevant in that it is the tone of the voice that the horse will respond to, not the word itself. We once did an experiment with a young horse on the lunge substituting the word 'cheese' for 'walk', and it seemed that as long as it was used in a drawn-out fashion it mattered little to the horse that the actual word used was not 'walk'; it was the association that mattered.

This does not mean, however, that any words might be used willy-nilly, because consistency is of vital importance if the horse is not eventually to feel confused. So if 'cheese' is to be substituted for 'walk', then it should be used from that point on.

Horses learn words of command very quickly and often respond to them in spite

Horses often listen to the voice of the trainer rather than their own rider. This can be useful in a teaching situation and proves their ability to recognize words of command.

of their rider's aids. Presumably this is because they first learned to obey the voice from the ground, aids being learnt later. As a trainer, I have nearly always found that when I give a rider an instruction, the horse hears me, and will respond before an aid is given by the rider. I may say to the rider who is cantering, 'When you get to B do a transition to . . .', and before I can say 'trot', the horse has brought himself to that pace. It is therefore obvious that making a definite impression in the horse's mind causes him to recall it very quickly.

> The voice can also have a very 'calming' effect: thus if you say 'Good boy' in a soothing tone the horse will almost instantly relax. On the other hand of the voice is used sharply, the horse becomes alert.

The Whip as an Aid

The use of the whip for gaining the horse's attention as well as for reprimanding him is very important. *How* the whip is used is just as important, too, because there should be a distinct difference in the horse's mind between asking him to pay more attention to a question, or punishing him because he has been disobedient. This point itself needs clarification.

Some horses are frightened of a whip. But to be afraid is no good to them. To gain the right effect in training, sufficient pain must be inflicted that there is a reaction of some kind. Some horses respond quickly to this kind of stimulus, others are much slower. Once a reaction occurs the horse should be praised.

> All modifications of behaviour and learning receptivity are obtained by adjusting the patterns of reward and punishment. Each owner should very quickly learn which pattern leads to the fastest learning and the fewest errors.

When he has learned to respond, the owner must decide whether the response he made was adequate. This lesson is important, because if the horse understands that the whip is being used to make him more alert he will also accept its further use to increase attention or to make him physically more active.

Punishment is a separate issue, and if the whip is used because the horse has been disobedient he should learn that in this circumstance its use will give him pain.

The Role of the Voice and the Whip in Training

It is crucial from everyone's point of view that the initial question asked of the horse is clear: first of all in our own mind, and then presented to the horse in an equally clear fashion. This can only be done if the horse owner has sufficient knowledge in the first place, and follows it by practical application.

We all know how much there is to learn and that one never stops learning, but there are some people who fail to keep an open mind and persist in following their own rules. One thing is certain when dealing with horses, and that is that there are no set rules; there are guidelines, but every horse is an individual and should be

This is the correct position for 'leading', but it is wise to carry a whip in the left hand in case it is needed.

When teaching a horse to lead, it is important for his own safety as well as yours that he learns to behave, and it is wise to carry a whip in case it is needed. When being lunged or long-reined he is learning the basics of his work for the future and this generally cannot be achieved without the help of a lungeing whip used correctly.

treated as such. Because of this individuality each will have its own sensitivity. Some are dull; others bright; each will respond to a question in a slightly different way and need different handling.

To return to the matter of giving the horse a question to answer. Much will depend on how it is asked. If it is presented in a clear consistent manner an answer should be expected. Some horses will be alert or intelligent enough to give one, others may not. For those who do not, the question may need to be reiterated more firmly together with the whip, which should be used definitely and with clear intention. On receiving this message the horse should 'wake up' and give the rider a reply. If he does not, the question should be repeated; if he does he receives praise from the voice.

In the circumstance of a deliberately obstructive answer, the person on the ground may try and drive home his authority by using his voice sharply or more deeply, together with a further flick from the whip. Forms of punishment will vary depending on the circumstance. A small misdemeanour is different to something obviously anti-social or possibly dangerous.

A small misdemeanour is when the horse has made a mistake in his interpretation of the aids. Anti-social behaviour is active opposition to the rider's wishes, such as napping. A failure to respond quickly enough to a question is less of a mistake than when it is ignored.

To conclude, I have observed considerable misuse of whips over the years, and it is important to remember that the whip was invented to help the rider to train the horse, *not* to frighten it!

Early Training from the Saddle

When riding, the means of making one's wishes known to the horse is by the aids given with the legs, hands and body-weight. When the horse is 'backed' he will learn to associate the voice, which he already understands, with the rein aids which he partly understands from having been lunged and long-reined.

To begin with, his balance will be displaced by the unaccustomed weight of the rider, so many of his responses may be interfered with. If a rider is secure in the saddle this interference will occur less often than with one not so secure, but it is understandable that the horse may have a problem to start with.

This horse is clearly not answering his rider's leg aids and the whip is needed to stimulate a response.

It is my experience that many riders are under the misapprehension that horses are born knowing the aids!

The most difficult thing for the horse to comprehend is the use of the leg aids: their pressure means nothing and indeed may barely be felt. In order to stimulate the horse sufficiently to respond when the leg aids are applied, the whip is employed. Thereafter it is important that it is used only to assist the leg aids, *not* to replace them.

Many trainers use spurs to teach the horse to respond to leg aids but this should only be done to 'fine tune' an aid, and only a knowledgeable person should use them. I have never found that they are any substitute for a whip used correctly when teaching the horse.

All the natural aids available – voice, weight, hands, legs – have to be used in a coordinated fashion to be effective; if they are not used in this way the message the horse receives may well be fragmentary and this will confuse him.

Good coordination of the aids comes from a rider being able to maintain a steady contact with the horse's sides with the legs, and with his mouth with the hands via the reins. This contact should be consistent so that the horse does not receive intermittent messages.

When an aid is given the horse's brain receives it, interprets it, and then passes it on to those areas of his body that are required to answer. If he receives an intermittent message he will not have time to interpret it, or he may be confused as to its meaning. For whatever reason, he will not be able to respond in the desired way.

This process of the rider's aids being transmitted to the horse, and his response, should be understood in order that the rider may make allowance for any delays. The rider must first decide on his own plan of action. This thought is then transferred from the brain to the necessary muscles and ligaments that cause the limbs to function. Only then can they respond and give the original thought message to the horse. Following all this the horse then has to go through the same process. It should be made clear, therefore, that responses cannot be given nor answered without due preparation followed by a time delay.

As understanding between rider and horse develops the coordinated use of the rider's aids, and the replies given by the horse become more closely knit. In fact if a particular rider and horse train together for a long time their work becomes almost telepathic, with minimal signals being passed and readily understood. A situation of anticipation is then present in the horse's mind, which necessarily must be controlled by the rider's own anticipation of the horse's probable action.

It is always important to remember that the horse's power of memory is exceedingly high: once he has been taught something he will never forget it. This is an invaluable attribute in his training, although it can work against the rider if the horse should learn the wrong thing.

To anticipate his probable action in a situation the rider must appreciate that if he has taught the horse something particular in a specific place the horse will remember, and may expect to be asked. His mind will be warning him of a probable outcome and he will prepare himself.

As riders we are often involved in our own thoughts, and are not reckoning on

> It is so important that all our signals to the horse are absolutely clear and positive. Negative or weak aids are, to the horse, like a crackling telephone conversation is to us.

the horse's anticipation; and so a moment of confusion may arise.

The Training Environment

When teaching the ridden horse in the early stages it is important that this is done in an atmosphere in which he will concentrate and be most receptive. If he can see other horses galloping about in a field nearby, or if there are distractions such as children or dogs, his mind will be on them rather than on what you are trying to tell him via the aids. Having said that, sometimes these situations should be created intentionally as a learning exercise to teach concentration – but only when you are ready.

It is also pointless to try to school any horse on ground that is unsuitable. He cannot balance properly if he is having to go continually up and down hill (although this may be done for a purpose later on), and if he is slipping about or getting bogged down in deep going he will become harassed and fed up.

A good environment for training which includes a safe surface, suitable fencing and protection from the weather from banks and hedges.

Physical Needs
Always remember that even if the mind is willing the horse cannot function effectively unless it is physically able. It is essential therefore to maintain the animal's condition at a level consistent with the work he has to do (see Chapter 8).

Throughout his life the horse will, from fear or insecurity, display negative thoughts in his reaction to certain situations. As owners it is essential to help him through those moments when he is worried. We should encourage him to do those things he believes he cannot do and support him as a friend and partner. He will draw much strength from this union and will rely on it in his daily work.

Man's Response

Discipline is as essential to the horse as to its owner. Self-discipline for the rider is hard, but it is necessary if he is to be successful. Regarding obedience, I have found that total domination is not the answer, whereas total cooperation is: to make a horse obey without resentment can be exceedingly difficult, but an unwilling partner can never create the sort of harmony one seeks. Firm handling without cruelty, praise for small improvements and above all patience, will lead you in the right direction.

Whatever you are teaching the horse – whether it is how to do a figure-of-eight or jump a six-foot fence – *begin at the beginning*, take time, and always remember that laying a sound foundation is essential if you wish to build upon it!

CHAPTER 5

Curiosity and Conflict

The horse is necessarily a curious creature. In the wild this trait is important for his survival, when investigation of an unusual or unknown smell, sight or sound is vital to his safety. He possesses inborn fears which motivate him to suspect all kinds of things that we may not expect him to; the scent of other animals for instance would come high on the list. Knowing his history we can accept this as entirely reasonable and therefore should make allowances for proper introductions.

Investigation of any new odour or strange object is of prime importance in order to eliminate it from the 'danger' category, even if it is on the horse's home territory. Thus the brand-new mounting block, the rejuvenated post and rails or the water butt that has changed position will cause enormous consternation, but these initial anxieties are usually followed by a strong urge to have a closer look.

A loose horse in a field often takes some time to come within touching range of whatever is bothering him. He may approach, but feeling suddenly unsure of himself will gallop off – only to return for another look. He may edge up slowly step by step, neck outstretched, so that should he detect danger he is still able to turn and run. If his senses tell him the object is harmless he may eventually lick it or even bite it to be quite sure of its safety, and also to find out if it is edible, a matter of prime interest.

This is the horse's instinctive approach, and we should expect this sort of behaviour when riding or leading him when he sees, smells or hears something which frightens him. We should also appreciate that even though he may be fearful, he will not be satisfied until he is sure in his own mind of the harmlessness of the object that is bothering him, so it is pointless to fight with him or to become impatient. If he is allowed to have a good look while being given firm reassurance he will get over his worry.

Curiosity leads horses into many scrapes and awkward situations, and the younger the animal the more inquisitive he will be. Everything must be investigated and summed up, and he will then either dismiss it as of no importance, or determine that it should be avoided at all costs.

Young foals are innately inquisitive and cannot resist looking at anything new,

---

Foals are very adept at getting on the opposite side of the fence to their mothers, which of course sends everyone into a furore. We have consistently found that horses seem to have no problem at all in finding an open gate when we would prefer them not to, but can never find it in moments such as this!

---

although their curiosity often exceeds their sense. One foal we owned, curious to see if a handleless rubber bucket was edible, took it up in his teeth; frightened by it he then galloped off, but forgot to let it go! He rushed about in quite a panic until eventually he *did* let it drop – by which time we were also in a nervous state!

A horse in panic can be very frightening, particularly, in my opinion, when it gets caught up for example in a fence. This normally occurs because it wants to see or to reach whatever is on the other side, though it only realizes it is caught when it starts trying to retreat. Flight from such a trapped situation is the horse's first thought, and if this is impossible he will try to fight his way out of it. His own size

is often a handicap, so that the more he struggles the more trapped he becomes. Horses of different natures will, however, react differently: thus some may kick and thrash about causing great harm to themselves and to anyone trying to rescue them, whereas others will lie or stand quite quietly until someone comes to extract them.

The surprising thing is that such a terrifying experience does not necessarily cure curiosity, and an animal will often get himself in the same muddle again if we do not take preventative measures.

Curiosity combined with herd instinct may also cause trouble, such as when one horse is turned out alone in a field and another is ridden past. The one in the field wishes to join the other, probably chiefly

Natural inquisitiveness does lead horses into trouble. Owners should be on the alert for such dangers.

for company but also out of curiosity, so much so that he jumps the fence into the road, causing all manner of hazards to himself and road users.

A curious horse will paw with a forefoot, an action used instinctively as a way of testing or exploring new objects; in the wild it would make a water-hole larger, and a horse still does it to prepare a site on which to roll. When pawing at objects, however, he risks getting his foot caught, and he may well pull off a shoe or injure himself or even get caught and be unable to move. Again, feeling trapped he will fight to get away and may as a result cause himself further injuries.

Boredom combined with curiosity may lead a horse to find out how to let himself out of his stable. Horses can seldom resist fiddling with almost any object and door bolts are very tempting. Once the horse has got out in this way he will repeat the experiment and will soon discover exactly how to do it. We had one clever fellow who, finding his own bolt 'clipped' to prevent him escaping, actually jumped the partition (some 3ft 6in high) between his stable and the next and opened his friend's bolt instead, a quite remarkable achievement!

The feed room is inevitably an attraction, but it may also be curiosity that makes a horse try every bag or bin he can get at. Not everyone has a bin for every single foodstuff, so not only will a large amount of food be wrecked, but the horse may well give himself colic, too. A particular danger is unsoaked sugar beet which if ingested will swell inside the animal causing colic or even death.

Why the Horse Feels Conflict

Frustration

One of the main causes of conflict in a horse's mind arises when we don't allow him to do what he wants. Perhaps he is being led and we prevent him joining a friend he sees in the distance. His urgent desire for company is prompted by his primitive 'group' instinct, and preventing him from fulfilling that desire can result in a great deal of anxiety or even display of temper. Most horse owners have probably been trampled on or nearly knocked over in this sort of situation!

Similarly, perhaps we won't allow our horse to join its companions in a race: we frustrate his purely natural desire to gallop with others and he cannot understand why. In this sort of situation his mind becomes totally confused and he will very likely throw himself about quite out of control.

Strength

In normal circumstances the horse's natural strength will enable him to get his own way. Throughout his early life he will test this strength against any obstacle that he feels is obstructing him, be it his stable door, the paddock fence or maybe his owner. Therefore one of the earliest

Water will frequently intrigue a horse. We had an automatic system installed and our horse was so fascinated by the hissing sound of water trickling into the bowl that he kept pressing the lever until eventually the stable was flooded! Another time one of the ponies did the same with the ballcock in the water trough in the field, having first dislodged the lid covering it!

lessons he has to learn is to control his strength and natural desires. When he is calm the horse will quite happily accept the idea of being frustrated in his aims; but once he is tense his thinking becomes muddled and he may behave foolishly. In fact there is almost nothing strong enough to contain a horse if it is determined to reach its goal, and it will go over, under or through almost anything.

The Wish to Please

Many horses are very genuine in their wish to please, yet this desire can also lead to feelings that conflict. One such was a most willing animal, always happy to learn, but so much so that she would always try to anticipate the next move. Inevitably this caused friction because she had to be checked, sometimes many times as she made the same mistake over and over again. This kind of circumstance leads to the horse feeling great anxiety as it tries to puzzle out exactly what its rider wants.

An alarmed horse may suffer a high degree of inner conflict too, if his fear challenges his desire to obey his rider. Take a horse executing a dressage test where a high level of obedience is present in his mind. He is intent on listening to his rider, but suddenly notices a black plastic bag on a nearby post. He is instantly distraught because his senses tell him that the object is of potential danger, and yet he must do what his rider tells him; one part is telling him to pay attention, the other to turn and run.

Laziness

Idleness can be a considerable handicap to attaining a goal. In short, some horses are

There are some horses which want to be friendly but are too worried by past experience to allow this to happen.

I once owned a pony which when we bought her seemed to be the most friendly creature in the world, but she turned out to have a decidedly different side to her nature. In the stable she was very docile, but when she was put out in the field she acted very differently. When we called her to catch her in, she would come rushing across with her ears pricked apparently eager to be caught, but as soon as she was close enough she would turn and kick out at us quite viciously! Our interpretation of this odd behaviour was that although basically she had a nice nature, she had almost certainly experienced much unpleasantness at the hands of humans and was not going to give anyone the chance to treat her in such a way again.

It was fortunate that in her case the abuse she had suffered had not completely destroyed her nature. Others are not so lucky.

simply too lazy to put in the effort required. Maybe they do quite want to please, but can't be bothered; in which case it is up to *us* to take the initiative. Coercion is the likely answer!

Active Resistance

There are many occasions when the horse decides he does not want to obey us, and actively obstructs us. Perhaps he finds it frightening, or difficult or painful – but whatever the reason, his brain tells him not to do it. Of course he knows that ultimately he will have to do what his owner wants, but he resists for as long as he can, his resistance no doubt fuelled by the knowledge that we may use force to make him give in. He will not be happy about this, and although he will eventually obey, if he finds himself in the same situation again he may suffer the same dilemma.

If his dislike is handled with tact, however, he may come to accept it, or even to get over it. Much will depend on the sensitivity of his owner.

Man's Response

As owners we should always anticipate trouble or problems – yet even the most knowledgeable person will not be successful in this every time. Nevertheless we must try to be careful in all our dealings with the horse, and should constantly use our imagination to anticipate problem areas. Horses will get themselves into trouble one way or another, but we must try to avoid putting them in situations where they can hurt themselves. Potential hazards include wire and metal fence posts, boulders with jagged edges, inaccessible corners of fields, tree stumps, buckets with handles, stables with low doors – these are just some that the owner of the curious horse will have to consider.

Also if we can understand how a horse's desires may conflict in his mind we may be in a better position to help him come to terms with them.

CHAPTER 6

Physical Structure and Movement

The physical construction of the horse is relevant to his psychological state in that if the structure in any way makes it difficult for the horse to do what his owner wants it will affect his willingness and mental attitude.

Conformation

The most obvious aspect of the horse is his external physical build. Clearly perfect conformation would be an asset both to the horse and to us, but this attribute is rare. We can train ourselves to spot faults fairly easily; there are several that are more of a hindrance than others to the horse, and some may even cause injury or disease.

Study the horse's skeleton and it is apparent that there is a good deal more weight from the saddle forwards than behind it because of the shoulder blades, ribs, neck and head. Thus it is clearly more desirable to have a well proportioned horse, and not one that is built more on the forehand than is necessary. By this I mean that a horse with a **neck** that comes forwards or downwards from the withers instead of upwards is less easy to train, as are those which are built with a rise to the loin. Such horses are inevitably handicapped for training purposes, especially

with the weight of the rider, and however willing they may be, they will find it very difficult to perform as required.

The **shoulder** blade should slope and not be upright, and its set is very important as it affects the action and scope of the horse.

A large **head** could be a problem, as the horse may not be able to carry it in the way the rider wants.

Because the weight of the horse is primarily in his forehand, it is important to his balance when he is ridden for the rider to 'engage' his **hindquarters** under his body, as this helps to lift and therefore lighten the forehand. A horse with a long back will find this procedure even more difficult, and any weakness in the hindquarters themselves will compromise the horse's ability to produce the necessary power to drive himself forwards. Horses that are heavy in front and/or weak behind will always have trouble in going correctly, particularly over fences.

The structure of the **limbs** is crucial: they must be of the right substance and bone to support the horse, and the joints in particular must be strong as they will have to take so much strain throughout the horse's life. Weakness of the limbs can cause lameness: bony enlargements such as splints or spavins may develop, and

Although this horse's head may be a little large, he should have no problems in training as it is well joined to the neck.

The withers of this horse are rather high which can present a problem to the fitting of the saddle.

A straight hind leg, as shown in this picture, can affect action as well as performance. In addition this horse shows the sort of shaped neck that is very difficult to bring into a good outline.

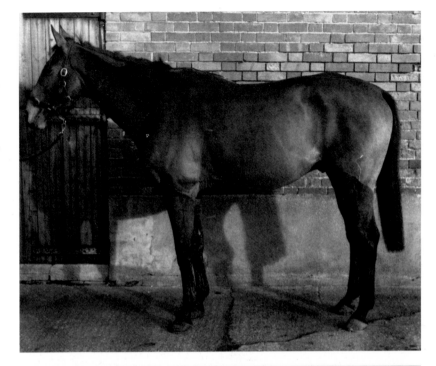

Horses who are built 'high behind' have difficulty in lowering the hindquarters as required in training.

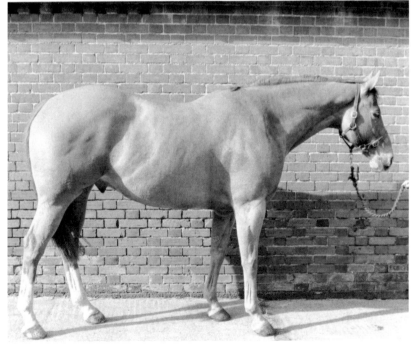

A large or heavy head, especially if it is combined with a short thick neck, can be a problem in training.

there could be a tendency towards sprains of tendons or fetlocks.

The **feet** are of great importance. Hooves should be deep and wide between the heels; narrow or boxy feet restrict the physiological function of the foot and may lead to disease such as navicular or pedalostitis. A lame horse, for whatever reason, will never be a happy one.

The Digestive System

We are taught to feed our horses 'little and often' as their digestive system copes best with such a routine. If we do not follow this rule we undoubtedly put their health at risk and so also threaten their content-ment. We also need to know *what* they need, because if we deprive them of essen-tial elements their operative powers will be reduced.

These elements are as follows:

Carbohydrates: Energy-producing organic compounds containing carbon, starch and oxygen eg starch, glucose and other sugars.

Proteins: Essential constituents of all living cells. They are of animal or vegetable origin and break down the amino acids during digestion, and are vital for growth, maintenance and repair of the body.

Fats: Basically stored food reserves of the body, used for heat and energy.
Water: Essential to all life.
Vitamins: Important dietary additives, essential to normal health and development.
Minerals: Vital to life and required in constant supply.
Trace Elements: Important, but required in smaller amounts.

The last three are all involved in the chemical processes that sustain life.

In the wild the horse would naturally find all these elements for himself by eating vegetation, bark and even soil. In domesticity we must make good this loss in order to keep him healthy enough to do the work we want him to do. A healthy horse is a happy horse.

The Teeth

Many horses suffer because their owners do not look after their teeth. Grave discomfort is often caused because they fail to notice that young horses are losing their milk teeth or that adult teeth are forming incorrectly. Not only can this affect a horse's appetite and subsequent condition, it can also be the cause of problems when the horse is ridden (see Chapter 12). The back molars may develop sharp edges, particularly in the older horse, and these will need filing down by a vet; otherwise the horse will find it increasingly difficult to grind his food properly, predisposing to colic and lack of condition.

Horses will eat contentedly side by side as these two are, but often one will bully the other who will end up getting left out. Care should be taken to give foodstuffs that suit the age and size of the animal.

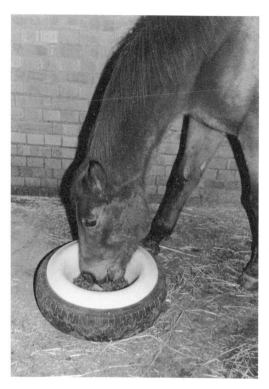

Placing feeding bowls in a rubber tyre is a good way to prevent their being overturned and food wasted.

Of course small ponies cannot have haynets out of reach but this net being hung so low will most certainly cause a pawing forefoot to become trapped.

The Mouth

The shape of a horse's mouth may affect his reaction to the bit. For instance a horse with a very small mouth will have less room for the bit to lie and it may therefore be uncomfortable. A parrot mouth or an undershot jaw can also pose problems which may make the horse actively resist his rider.

The Respiratory System

There are many conditions that may affect the horse physically and in consequence also mentally. A horse which is asked to work when he is coughing for example will suffer distress and be uncooperative. Horses which are not fit enough for their work will be unable to respond adequately.

Bridles that are badly fitted, throat lashes that are too tight or nosebands that inhibit the nostrils are all unfair to the horse as they can adversely affect his breathing.

If a horse is unwell he may 'blow' excessively, an abnormality which should be quickly recognized as such by the owner. Sometimes a less knowledgeable person is concerned when a horse snorts rhythmically as he works; this is known as 'high blowing' and is not abnormal, nor is the horse distressed by it. 'Whistling' and 'roaring' are conditions which generally result from partial paralysis of the left vocal cord; neither condition affects performance. They are, however, hereditary.

The Nervous System

The central nervous system is composed of the brain and spinal cord. Movement, function and sensation result from a message being sent from the central nervous system to the relevant organs or limbs.

Every part of the body is supplied with nerves from the brain or spinal cord; these may be split into three main categories:
1. Motor nerves regulating movement.
2. Sensory nerves registering sensation.
3. Automatic nerves controlling the bowel, blood and heart.
The first two are the only ones that the horse owner need to be concerned with; the third is outside voluntary control.

Many of the responses that the horse makes are of his conscious choosing, but many are reflex actions made automatically by the nervous system. For instance, the blinking of an eyelid is a reflex action, whereas the horse shying as a result of what he sees should be considered as his choice.

The Reproductive System

Owners of mares should understand the normal 'cycles' which to a greater or lesser extent may affect behaviour. The normal breeding season is to a certain extent related to grass and light. During the dark days of winter when fodder in the wild is seriously restricted the oestrous period is suppressed. However, if the weather is mild in January, or the mare is stabled in simulated spring conditions, she may well come in season, and may be covered.

The usual length of a mare's cycle is twenty-one days between ovulations, although this does vary. The length of the season varies with the time of year but can be anything from three weeks to six days as the year goes by. Ovulation usually occurs about twenty-four hours before the end of the season.

A mare in season will usually give obvious signs of her state, although there are some who seem completely unaffected. She will 'show' to a stallion, and may even do so to a gelding, by straddling her back legs and issuing secreta from the vagina. Sometimes this demonstration is quite excessive, and it may be a positive nuisance when the mare is ridden. Although it is a natural reaction the rider should take a firm line so that she learns that such behaviour is not permissible while she is being ridden. Most will accept this, although some make more fuss than others.

Mares do sometimes suffer from problems relating to the ovaries. These are attached to the roof of the abdomen just in front of the pelvis, and if there is some problem the mare may show her discomfort by constantly bucking or kicking out. In this circumstance the owner should seek veterinary advice.

The Kidneys

The two kidneys are situated in the lumbar region of the back in front of the pelvis. They are of course crucial to the horse's good health and should therefore be treated with care. When riding it is important that this area does not receive too much weight, either from a badly fitted saddle or an overweight or insensitive rider. Horses may demonstrate their objections by sinking their back when being mounted, or by standing with their legs somewhat straddled while at halt.

Muscle Development

Only from a basically correct frame can a correct, effective muscle structure develop, and only with this development can the horse do what we want. Muscle is essential for supporting the frame, and failure to comprehend and strive for this will result in disappointment with the horse's performance. It is therefore most important that a gradual build-up takes place by using appropriate exercises when riding (see Chapter 12). It is also essential to realize that the horse can only co-operate if he is strong enough to do so.

It is up to us to give him that chance.

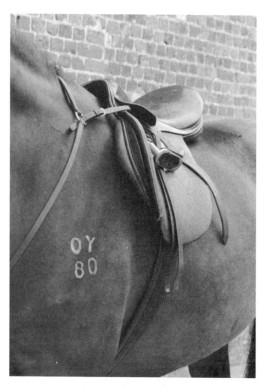

It is sometimes necessary to use a breast plate to keep a saddle in the right place. This prevents it from slipping back towards the vulnerable area of the

The Limitations of a Horse's Physique

The successful owner will be the one who has studied his horse's framework and then asks it to do no more than it is capable of doing.

One point to bear in mind is that although the horse can arch himself longitudinally to a high degree, he cannot do so to the same extent laterally. His backbone is in fact virtually rigid from the withers to the tail, and although we may talk about a 'bend through the horse' this relates mainly to the movement of the shoulders, neck and hindquarters. It is chiefly muscular suppleness that gives the horse the appearance of bend.

Hereditary Problems

Just as temperament can be inherited, so can faults in conformation. It is wise therefore when breeding to avoid producing animals that may throw a particular fault. Any imperfections can result in problems for the horse, which could cause behavioural difficulties.

This grand-looking horse shows muscle development over his 'topline', his second thigh and forearm, all essential to efficient performance.

Movement

In order to appreciate difficulties relating to movement it is important to know something about the gaits. In all basic gaits the horse's hind feet should follow in the tracks of the forefeet. If they do not, there may be a fault in conformation; his muscle development may be uneven; or if under saddle, the horse may be resisting his rider for some reason (he may be in pain). All gaits should show regularity of stride, meaning that the horse should take steps of equal length or height to each other.

Each gait has its own sequence of steps: the walk is four-time, the trot is two-time and the canter three-time. The gallop is also four-time.

In trot, the horse brings one pair of diagonal legs to the ground and then the other with a moment of suspension in between.

In canter there is a moment of suspension after each three-beat stride.

When the horse is going in a balanced way there should be a clear rhythm in each gait.

Irregularities of the gaits are usually due either to lameness or poor training.

The horse's attitude to being ridden,

Clearly this animal is reluctant to work although the flexion of his hind legs shows he is capable.

The upright position of the off hind shows that the horse's hindquarters are insufficiently engaged and because of this he is 'on the forehand'.

This horse is displaying a very 'flat' gait and is going 'into the ground', rather than springing off it.

driven or simply shown in hand may well be affected by the way he moves, particularly if he is at all limited in ability. Ideally he should have a lot of scope, freedom of the shoulders and a good ground-covering stride. If he has the right frame these things will be possible; if, however, he is long in the back, or has an upright shoulder, or is perhaps cow-hocked or has a weak second thigh, he will be handicapped. Some horses do manage to break all the rules, moving well in spite of incorrect structure.

For dressage the horse must be able to bend his joints and move with great flexibility. For showing he needs flowing and graceful action which should also be straight when viewed both from in front and behind. To jump successfully in competition he must be very athletic. Not only should his limbs be strong, they should be constructed so that he can move without dishing or turning in his toes; these problems may affect him adversely, because he will find it harder to go in a straight line and to control his actions

Apart from showing some resistance to the bits this horse appears happy and looks as though he is working well.

properly, and is more likely to become unbalanced or to trip.

The strength of the hindquarters is particularly important since it is in the quarters that all the propelling energies are stored, those that the horse needs to drive himself forwards. Also hind legs that come well under the quarters in work are a far greater asset than hind legs which trail along behind and whose action dramatically reduces power.

Man's Response

In order to have a full picture of our horse's psychological reactions we need to study his physiology and everyday functions. It is pointless to feel discouraged or to blame the horse for being uncooperative if the truth is that he is simply unable physically to carry out our demands. When you encounter problems, try putting yourself in the horse's place and you may find greater understanding of what he is going through mentally; this process will frequently provide a solution.

The Suitability of Different Breeds for Different Disciplines

Type	Characteristics	Capability	Rider
Thoroughbred	Sensitive and highly strung; prone to anxiety; quick to learn	Bred to race. Suitable for eventing, dressage and showing (subject to conformation)	Knowledgeable, experienced, sensitive, not a novice
Arabian	High-spirited, intelligent, independent, full of stamina	'In hand' showing, endurance riding, racing. General riding	Sensitive, knowledgeable, not a beginner's ride
Warmbloods Swedish, Dutch, German, etc	Less sensitive than the TB; can lack speed. Vary in size and weight. Temperaments vary but tend to be steady. Often need strong riding	Mainly dressage and show jumping	Should match the horse in size, and be a strong rider. Not usually a beginner's ride
Coldbloods Shires, Percheron, Clydesdale, etc	All heavily built. Intended for draught work. If crossed with TB can produce useful hunters or riding horses. Generally not suitable for gymnastic work	Hunting, general riding	Not usually suitable for small people as tend to be rather wide
Native Ponies Shetland, Exmoor, Dartmoor, New Forest, Highland, Welsh, etc	Vary in height and width; independent. Wide ones can be difficult to fit saddle. Welsh have lively temperaments	Good children's ponies if correctly broken and schooled. Can be used for any job	Novices and the more expert
Crossbreeds Mixed breeds such as native/cob, or draught crossed with TB or Arab	Vary enormously from ponies to big horses. Temperaments will also cover a wide range	Should be of a suitable height and have the physical ability to do the job required. Unlikely to be suitable for racing	Must fit the horse; rider and horse must suit each other in temperament

PART TWO

CHAPTER 7

The Effects of Restrictive Stable Management

A horse is essentially a 'free' animal which reacts instinctively by flight if he feels threatened or in danger. In the wild his natural lifestyle would be to roam at will over large areas, grazing, on the move for twenty-four hours of the day. As soon as he is deprived of his natural inclinations he may seek to relieve his fears or boredom in a variety of ways; in particular limiting his territory and freedom to range will subject him to all kinds of frustrations. He will develop anxieties, tensions, even bad temper, and may get himself into serious trouble.

As the horse is by instinct a herd animal one of his basic needs is for companionship. This may come from a human or from another species of animal, and he will almost certainly find the presence of a person, dog or another horse most comforting. We have nearly always owned several horses at one time and I believe they have been happier because of it. They

> The following story demonstrates the inherent need horses have for each other and their apparent contentment while together. We had one particular little native pony, Lucky, who chose another mare in the field, Chance by name, as her friend. They were inseparable and were always almost within touching distance. Chance was sometimes disagreeable to poor Lucky who tried to share her feed bin and even the blade of grass she was eating! She often got bitten or kicked as Chance retained the lion's share. When they were being caught it was quite unnecessary to catch Lucky as she would not be separated for anything. This was particularly awkward if her rider wished to go somewhere away from Chance, in fact it was impossible! The two ponies lived together and frequently escaped from their field together until the day Chance died of old age; at which point Lucky retired to the other end of the field and became instantly attached to someone else!

Attention Seeking

Some horses develop habits to draw attention to themselves; this may be because they are hungry or thirsty, but it is just as likely that they are bored and are seeking companionship. Banging the stable door with a forefoot is perhaps the most common, and as a rule it sufficiently irritates owners into going to see what the horse wants. Generally it is because the haynet is empty or the horse has knocked over the water bucket.

We had one horse that was not at all violent but just tapped quite gently on the door whenever it was time for exercise or she was short of food. This might happen

Two ponies living together can become almost inseparable, which can cause difficulties when one is taken out on its own.

do form particular attachments, and if living in a group one horse will often single out another as its special friend.

I also know of many 'one-horse' owners whose horse seems to appreciate the presence of a cat in the stable. Normally horses object to things touching their legs, yet they seem happy to tolerate a cat winding itself in and out around their feet, or spending hours perched contentedly on their backs or sleeping in the manger. And some horses obviously derive great reassurance from the sight or sound of their owners gardening or moving about in the house if this is within range.

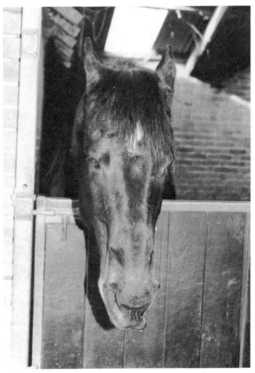

Boredom and 'sucking the tongue' may be the first steps towards a stable vice.

Restriction can lead horses to develop all manner of bad habits. Although both these animals appear calm, each has an expression of boredom. The one on the left looks as if he could be going to bang his door and the one of the right might easily chew the top of his.

even in the middle of the night but she knew that eventually someone would come to see what she wanted.

Young horses often develop the habit of door banging, and they should be told off for doing this; once they understand that they will be punished for it, they will generally stop just from the sound of the voice. It is not good practice to allow door banging because of the risk of injury, besides which it is an annoying habit; and if it does happen, owners should consider whether their horse is having sufficient exercise or interest in his life, as opposed to merely being naughty.

Pawing the stable floor or digging up the bed can also be a call for attention although it may also be because the horse is craving more chance to exercise. Horses that have been cooped up for long periods may well develop this habit.

Pawing may be associated with colic or other forms of illness so this must be considered before deciding on a course of action. Most horses paw as a preliminary to rolling, and this is entirely natural. If a horse is stabled all the time he is not getting the same opportunity to roll which he would do in the field, so he may paw because he wants to roll, but then feels inhibited about actually doing so.

Rolling

Horses have an inborn compulsion to roll: by rolling the horse is able to scratch, remove sweat or itching loose hair, and to cover his coat with dust or mud which protects him from the weather. In the wild, rolling is also a statement of familiarity by one member of a herd to another.

A horse may roll to relieve tension. One of our horses would not roll in his box, but would paw the bed until someone turned him out into the paddock. He would then roll furiously for about five minutes, and once he was plastered, would come to the gate and ask to come back in. After that he was perfectly quiet in his stable for the rest of the day. However, if he was prevented from doing this each day, even when we were at a three-day show, he became quite hysterical and impossible to ride. There are probably many horses that need this relief.

Bucking and Kicking Out

In the stable this behaviour can be alarming and even dangerous, and is a sure sign of pent-up emotions that need to be released by violent physical expression. One of the ways in which horses exercise themselves when they are free is by galloping about or leaping around in various ways. Young horses certainly do this every day if they can, and although older stabled horses will have become used to a different way of life and may not feel the need so much, they too, must have some freedom sometimes.

Rolling is a natural action in order to scratch or, in some cases, relieve tension. Most horses roll daily especially after work.

Given a horse's natural instincts, it is clearly wrong to leave him in a stable without any means of regular exercise, whether this is by riding him or turning him loose in a field. He will quickly become fed up and start looking for ways to amuse himself or to relieve boredom.

Self-Amusement

Throwing buckets out of the stable or pushing a feed bin round the floor are ways in which a horse might entertain himself. However, in order to prevent the horse from inventing his own, possibly annoying ways to amuse himself, it is a good idea to provide him with a harmless 'toy' of some kind. This can be nutritious, such as a salt block or swede tied on a string suspended from a beam; alternatively some people give their horse a block of wood or rubber tyre to push about. This may serve a purpose, but it may lead to other habits such as cribbing (crib-biting).

Cribbing or Crib-Biting

Unfortunately some horses choose to relieve boredom by gnawing at anything wooden; if the stable is made of wood this can be especially annoying. In the wild, horses would chew bark or branches to correct any deficiencies in their normal diet, so this habit may be instinctive as

Chewing wood or other objects is a natural act but can lead the stabled horse into a vice impossible to stop.

well as emotional; but whatever its cause, it is difficult to prevent unless some other form of interest is supplied.

> We looked after a friend's horse once that was rather tall for the loosebox she had to go in. We kept hearing gnawing noises but could not see where she was chewing. One day we caught her in the act by which time she had almost eaten through the rafters holding up the roof!

Windsucking

Cribbing often leads to windsucking, an activity which may be discovered by accident but which becomes totally addictive. It is a recognized 'vice' in that it can cause interference with the digestive process and so be detrimental to the horse's health. Also another horse may, out of curiosity and the urge to copy, pick up the habit himself; and unless precautions are taken this can be passed on to others in the stable. And although windsucking may not actually be hereditary, it is plain that a foal may mimic its mother if she happens to have the habit.

Lack of sufficient food may well be one of the causes of windsucking: having foraged around unsuccessfully for anything edible, the horse then tests the next available object. Finding it inedible he plays around and discovers that sucking air is an interesting way to pass the time.

Horses often grip something with their teeth in order to windsuck and this results in wear of the incisors; but they can successfully gulp in air without holding on to anything. They may even do it on the bit while being ridden.

Windsucking is addictive and is detrimental to digestion and teeth. It is a habit also copied by others in the vicinity.

Unfortunately there is no cure. The only preventive measure that can be taken is to fit a windsucking strap: this is worn where the head joins the neck and prevents the horse being able to get himself in the position necessary to suck in the air.

Horses appear to be quite calm when cribbing or windsucking but because they have a 'boredom habit' they may very well develop others, too,

Weaving

Another distressing habit is that of weaving. This originates from feelings of anxiety or tension and is bad for the horse

This type of weaving grill is safe and effective in reducing, or preventing, this tiresome habit which is an expression of frustration or anxiety.

Horses that are forced to stand behind a door grilled in this way can feel very claustrophobic. Most are happier being able to see out but some, especially if they weave violently, may be better off in this situation.

in many ways. He will sway from side to side, usually over his stable door but in some cases elsewhere in the stable, or over a field gate. He may sway gently, using mainly his head and neck, or he may be quite violent, jumping from one front foot to the other.

Because he is worked up he frets off his condition; he will often not eat properly, he wears out his shoes and puts strain on his joints and tendons. Insufficient exercise may be one contributory factor to this condition; also an urgent natural desire to get out and join in with the others, particularly if they can be seen in the distance.

Highly strung horses are more likely to weave; it seems that the lazier the horse is, the less likely he is to try it.

This habit is also exceedingly catching, so weavers should be kept out of sight of

A weaving grill should be fitted to the stable door to discourage the horse in his activity. These are fairly successful, or at least reduce the opportunity the horse has to indulge in it.

others. Unfortunately this does not help the weaver himself, whose main problem is an urgent need for company. It may be helpful to keep another animal such as a goat or a donkey within sight; neither of these is likely to contract the habit.

Box Walking

This is also a very distressing condition brought about by far too restricted an environment. The horse walks in a circle round and round his stable, normally in one direction only, almost without let-up. Plainly this is bad for him mentally as he behaves in a stupefied fashion, really not knowing why he is walking, but being far too frustrated to stop. Not only does it ruin the bedding, it may also cause general strain, especially on limbs.

Some people put a rubber car tyre on the ground to deter the horse, but persistent box walkers will not be put off.

Rug Chewing

The chewing of rugs is largely another means of relieving frustrations, although some horses do seem to do it for fun; these and others may have developed the habit because at some point they were uncomfortable or too hot. One mare I knew obviously disliked being rugged altogether and would systematically tear any rug to shreds in just a few hours. She never appeared to be especially bored and always had a full net of hay, so we concluded that she just did not like the feel of a rug, perhaps feeling restricted in it.

My very first horse was just mischievous. He found out that if he pulled the rug forwards with his teeth and kept pulling,

Too much restriction may cause the horse to learn to box walk, a condition distressing both for himself and his owner.

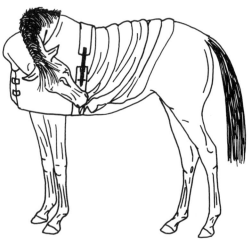

Horses pull off or chew their rugs for a variety of reasons and sheer frustration from boredom can be one.

This horse is wearing a bib which can help to restrict windsucking, cribbing or rug tearing. They should be kept clean as food tends to get stuck to them.

A muzzle is another way to stop a horse from indulging in stable vices such as cribbing. It is a nuisance from the point of view that it must be removed frequently to allow the horse to eat and drink.

it would gradually work its way through the roller and come off over his head. After that he would quite contentedly stand on it, making it as filthy as possible! He was the only horse I have known who managed to get out of a New Zealand rug with leg straps!

In an attempt to keep their rugs on I fitted both horses with a bib attached to their headcollar. This succeeded with the mare but the gelding still managed to get at the front of the rug, or to get the headcollar off! A proper cradle prevented his antics, but he looked so miserable we took it off. As he grew older he accepted his rugs

in cold weather, but he would remove them again once it became warmer.

Some horses will happily suck a corner of their rug, in the same way that a cow chews the cud. Presumably the rug is like a comforter to those who need it.

All manner of revolting-smelling substances can be bought to deter horses from attacking rugs, but these usually wear off after a while. Undoubtedly the problem sometimes begins because the rug fits badly, or because too many rugs have been used so the horse gets too hot. Also if mud or something itchy is trapped underneath the rug the horse will keep biting and scratching until he can appease the annoyance, even if he destroys the rug in the process. Many rug tearers probably start for this reason.

Bad Temper and its Causes

Frustration can find itself all manner of outlets, and the horse's individual inherited temperament will cause him to react in different ways, too. Any animal may become irritable if it is kept in a restricted environment: freedom is essential to all creatures. If the horse starts throwing a temper tantrum when you appear – such as putting his ears back, biting the top of the door, kicking or behaving in a generally threatening manner – the reason should be sought.

Highly strung horses are most easily upset, and if kept too contained may become extremely irritable. Furthermore getting cross with them is no good at all as this will only widen the gap in confidence already between you, and it may end up getting worse. These horses require understanding, and to be treated with sympathy. Naturally, however, they must not be allowed to think that they can do what they like. Any threatening behaviour should be corrected firmly, and when the horse accepts the reprimand he should be praised.

Rubbing the teeth against the top of a door or kicking at the wall are signs of annoyance or impatience. Although it may be necessary to correct the horse so that he knows that this is unsociable behaviour, a more useful course of action may be to find the cause of his impatience. The question to ask yourself is whether he has been shut away in his stable for too many

> The only way to get what you want from your horse is to make him your friend, and to teach him that you are his friend also. When you approach the horse he should look forward to seeing you – but this does not mean that you should always appear with a titbit as a bribe. Bad temper often occurs as a direct result of getting too many titbits which the animal then comes to expect, behaving badly when he does not get them.

hours, or whether you have left him waiting for his tea. Whatever the reason, it is up to you to find it.

In some ways idle horses can be even more bad-tempered than the highly strung ones. They do not like correction, and will often be surly and unwilling to co-operate. In order to gain a rapport, each owner must find his own answer, depending on the individual's response. Some will tolerate firm correction and need it; others respond better to more of a compromise.

We compromised with one particular mare. She had a most equable nature except when she was tacked up, when she became quite savage until all the tack was in place. Because we got to know that this was only temporary, and besides which because it was probably associated with some past experience – she had quite a few white hair patches where she had obviously had sores around her withers and girth – we did not punish her for this display of dislike.

Bad temper is generally born of human error. There is no reason why any horse should demonstrate anything other than natural aggression, which it is bound to show when it feels under pressure or

The following story is to show that unless they are correctly handled in the first place, horses can sometimes become dangerous.

I was once bitten in the back by a horse which had done the same thing to several other girls at the stables where I worked. Although he was tied up very short he somehow still managed to get me in a grip, holding on with frightening ferocity. I cannot begin to explain why he did this, apart from the fact that, clearly, he hated the human race and had found a way to show it. The sad outcome was that after a trial with the mounted police who got the same treatment, the horse eventually had to be put down. I feel sure that if that horse had been correctly punished the very first time it actually bit someone the ending might have been different.

thinks it is cornered. It is the way we handle it that takes it beyond its normal bounds. Confining a horse to a stable is in a sense cornering it. So long as it is quite happy with this arrangement there is no problem, but if it displays its dislike or unhappiness and we react tactlessly, then difficulties can arise. Once a horse has learned to display his temper there can only be an unpleasant outcome.

The Horse-Friendly Stable

As soon as we bring our horse into a restricted environment we are depriving him of the natural elements in his life, the chief one being the freedom to wander about exercising at will, and searching for food. It is therefore right and necessary that we make his life as pleasant as possible to make up for this loss. First of all he should have the maximum room available; it is clearly sensible not to restrict him more than necessary. A very small stable for his size, or a low roof, or a building that becomes too hot in summer, all these can make the horse miserable and desperate to get out. He should have enough room to walk about, to turn round easily and to roll if he wants to. He should have air and light, and if possible a view to look at. (See also Chapter 8.)

He should have plenty of food and water so that he is not driven to eating his bedding, or even his own droppings (only a few do this, but it is a disgusting habit and hard to eradicate). Most of all he should be given the opportunity to exercise on his own. If it is not possible to let him loose every day he should have the chance at least twice a week; even a tiny paddock will do. It is the feeling of freedom that is important.

The Horse-Friendly Paddock

Keeping horses in small paddocks for long periods is sometimes necessary if nothing else is available, but it can become a hazard. Horses soon become bored by the lack of grass keep and may then start to eat unsuitable, possibly poisonous vegetation, or to look for ways to escape. Overgrazed land is likely to carry a higher infestation of worms, meaning the horse will carry a greater worm burden, resulting in loss of condition.

In the winter, land becomes severely poached, especially around water troughs and in gateways, often causing horses to lose shoes, strain fetlocks or to contract mud fever.

Post and rail fencing is ideal, but plain wire – even when it is fixed in this way – can cause injury.

Suitable fencing is most important in order to minimize possible injuries resulting from horses leaning over or pawing, trying to reach food on the opposite side. Post and rail is generally accepted as the most suitable for horses, although this may need treating with creosote, as protection against being chewed.

Shelter must be provided if there is no natural cover in the field. This may be a purpose-built shed or a home-made one but it should be big enough for the number of animals needing to use it. Sometimes there is a problem if one animal tries to monopolize it, and refuses to allow others into it.

Fresh water should always be available. Stagnant water is unsuitable; it may be drunk, but as a rule horses will avoid it until fresh water is provided. Some people

Barbed wire should be avoided at all costs.

Stagnant water is unsuitable and this type of trough can be awkward to clean.

This traditional type of water trough is most suitable as the ballcock allows fresh water into the tank. However, ballcocks often need to be protected from enquiring noses or hooves.

It is useful to have some natural shelter in the paddock if no other shelter is provided.

deprive horses of water as a punishment for bad behaviour or because they believe it will make the horse more cooperative. This is a foolish and ill-conceived notion, and if such a practice is taken too far it could be exceedingly dangerous for the horse.

In any restricted situation such as a small paddock it is essential that adequate forage is provided if it is not available as keep. This is important both for the horse's state of mind and his physical condition, especially during the winter months when it will be in short supply.

Man's Response

Having taken away the horse's freedom it is our responsibility to treat him in a manner as much in accordance with his natural habits as possible. In order to keep him happy, and willing to do what we want, we should study his needs and provide them to the best of our ability.

CHAPTER 8

The Physical Needs of the Horse

It is a sad fact that many owners fail to realize how much the horse is affected mentally by his physical condition; although if we think about it rationally, no human or animal can function properly if he is not in good health. It is surprising therefore to find so many animals asked to perform which are in poor condition, unfit and miserable.

One horse I saw recently had a staring coat and was desperately thin, dragging itself round with its ears back and a depressed expression. Its owner was questioned as to its condition and expressed *surprise*! – apparently oblivious of the animal's feelings. This sort of ignorance is very distressing, and it is really pointless discussing a horse's psychology without first considering some of the essentials that a horse needs to keep him physically fit and therefore happy.

Environment

The first essential consideration if the horse is to be kept stabled is the size of the loosebox or stall. Unfortunately some horses have to be kept in stalls: while this may be necessary for the owner, stalls are certainly not a good idea for the horse as they are often narrow and sometimes dark, and they are undeniably boring

because he is staring at a blank wall with absolutely nothing to occupy his mind. If the horse is being exercised several times a day, as in a riding school situation, then a stall is not so bad for him. If he is not, he will become restless or even bad-tempered as a result of the restriction.

The Stable

A large, airy loosebox – minimum 12ft x 12ft (3½m x 3½m) – for an animal over 14.2hh, with plenty of light and a top door opening to the outside should provide ample opportunity for the horse to move about and keep interested.

The height and width of the doorways is important. A narrow passageway with a sharp turn into the stable may cause problems: some horses can cope quite well in narrow spaces, but others become very neurotic; thus a horse might feel that he cannot make the awkward turn and will quite soon begin to rush in order to get the procedure over quickly, risking slipping on the floor and perhaps banging himself on the doorpost. This sort of thing is very common, and generally speaking no horse should have to turn in order to get in or out of his stable: he should be able to go straight.

Many types of material are used in building a stable, the most common being timber or brick, both of which are suitable for horses. Corrugated iron is sometimes used because it is cheap but it has the disadvantages of being hot in summer and apt to drip with condensation in the winter.

All stables should be timber-lined to prevent injury caused by rolling or kicking the wall. Floors must not be slippery. Many owners take up the bedding during the day, leaving the horse with a hard surface to stand on and nowhere to lie down. Furthermore most horses like to lie down for a time during the day; it is a sign of trust in their owner and gives them necessary relaxation. An additional reason for providing bedding in the daytime is so that the horse feels he can urinate; many will not do so on concrete.

Bedding

There are many different types of bedding, and it should be chosen to suit the individual animal. For instance, a horse that suffers from respiratory problems should be bedded on dust-free material – although these are expensive, and unfortunately some owners only consider their pocket, and not their horse's health.

Bedding horses on deep litter is an accepted practice nowadays, and a perfectly acceptable one as long as the bed is managed properly. It is degrading for any horse, and also bad for their feet, to stand on a two-foot high layer of solid manure; often so much muck then sticks to hocks and elbows that it causes sores.

Water

This should always be available, and it should be changed at least once a day (three times would be better); if it becomes stale or covered in dust the horse may leave it, and it is essential that he drinks regularly. Some horses will not drink a great deal if the water is stale, and this is bad for them; ultimately it could result in dehydration. Electrolytes may be given: they play a part in holding water in solution in the blood, and can be added to the existing water supply; however, a bucket or waterbowl of plain fresh water should always be available too.

Food

As the horse's natural life is spent mostly eating, he may need other distractions when kept in a restricted environment where food may run out.

Bulk food such as hay fills the horse up and prevents him from getting up to mischief because he feels hungry. It replaces the natural herbage that he would choose for himself, and should be of reasonable quality. If he dislikes his diet a horse will go off his food, which then leads him to think about some other way of passing the time. Stable vices then become a possibility.

Horses will eat their bedding if they are not given enough food and some may do so anyway if they are particularly greedy. This may not be good for them, and in any case it may make them too fat – and a fat horse will not be any happier than a thin one as he struggles to do what his owner asks.

The horse needs certain vitamins and minerals in his diet and very occasionally these may have to be added as supplements in the normal food.

Short feeds will vary enormously depending on the age of the horse, his size and the work he is required to do. They

Hay keeps a horse occupied and is of course essential to his diet to replace natural fodder. Putting it in a rack is one method of feeding it.

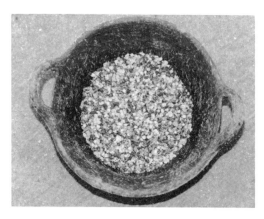

'Short feeds' can be mixed in a bowl such as this. They include nuts, oats, bran, chaff, maize, bruised barley, soaked sugar beet and other additives. Quantity depends on temperament, size, age and work being done.

may be based on oats, bran, chaff, sugar beet (always well soaked), crushed, rolled or flaked barley, flaked maize, horse cubes and other products. In addition the horse will need the following minerals: calcium, phosphorus and magnesium for bone formation, and salt to control body fluid levels, acidity and alkalinity. There are many others that occur in tissue structure, and all are necessary to the structural elements of the skeleton and teeth; they are also vital to the blood. Deficiencies can lead to rickets or similar conditions. However, the manufactured compound feeds currently available will provide all that are necessary and in proper proportion; otherwise an expert should be asked to advise.

Illness

Recognizing when the horse is not well is crucial to his physical and his mental well-being. Those in charge of horses should get to know them so intimately that they notice at once any change in behaviour. One of the signs to look for is how a horse stands in the stable: thus does he stand four-square, or does he constantly rest a particular leg? Is he alert? Do his ears prick when you come near, and does his eye look bright and clear? Always notice whether his nostrils are dry and whether his coat looks smooth and shining.

Grooming the horse is important to his health, but far more important is what he eats and how he looks. Every day he should be carefully checked for injury or abnormality – but mainly the owner will be able to tell how he is simply by looking at him.

Most experienced owners will glance into a field full of horses and be able to pick out any one that has something wrong with it; even from a distance it is possible to identify a swelling or other injury that will need attention.

Colic is a common illness and causes the horse much distress; pawing the ground or turning round to look at their sides, kicking out and so on may indicate colic. Sensible exercise and feeding help to prevent this happening. As already mentioned, the horse's digestive system requires that he eats little and often; if this rule were observed, many colic cases could be avoided.

A lot can be told about the horse's mental state by looking at his eye, especially if you know the horse well. It will register pain or apprehension quite obviously. Watching a horse breathe is also an

---

Vitamins are organic compounds that are necessary to the metabolism:

Vitamin A: Bone formation and vision – grass and vegetables.
Vitamin D: Assists bone formation – hay and fish oils.
Vitamin E: Important to muscular system – cereal, green plants and hay.
Vitamin K: Important to clotting mechanism of blood – hay and pasture.
Vitamin B: For cell metabolism – brewer's yeast and normal dietary substances.
Vitamin C: To keep a healthy epithelium (tissue forming outer layer of body surface) – apples and grass.

Salt may be added to short feeds or provided in block form.

Learning to keep horses in the right condition, giving them suitable quantities of food and preventing them from over- or under-eating is an art which is only learned with experience. It is most important that it is done correctly if the horse is to work properly and be happy doing so; if in doubt, ask the advice of an expert nutritionist.

Cod-liver oil is an excellent additive, although many horses do not like the smell of it. However, because it is so good for them it is worth disguising it in order to get them to eat it. This may be done by introducing something sweet such as treacle or apples.

---

indication of his health. Any differences from a normal regular steady breathing could mean that there is a problem. Also his dung will provide a clue. Any abnormalities should be noticed at once.

Worm Burden

Worming should take place on a regular basis, as once infestation takes hold it may be very difficult to eradicate. Horses can suffer a great deal if they have a heavy worm burden, both in condition and mentally if they feel off colour as a result. Rubbing the tail is an indication of infestation. Most preparations nowadays are easily given so there should be no reason not to keep up to date with doses.

One additional point on the subject is the importance of removing droppings from the paddock. This is especially relevant in restricted enclosures as they will quickly re-infect the ground if not taken away regularly. Pastures do become 'horse-sick' after a time; rotational grazing with other animals is always a good policy, as well as regular fertilization.

Viruses

Horses, like humans, are sometimes off colour but with no very evident symptoms. Lethargy, and disinterest in food and life in general should be sufficient to make owners realize that something is wrong. Viruses are often obscure, and they have to take their course in any case, which may take some time. It is no use rushing the horse back into work before he is ready, and even then he may need a week or two before he feels fit enough for work.

Horses which have been made to work too quickly following a virus take a long time to 'come right'. Their listlessness is often ignored by unsympathetic owners, although this is something they subsequently regret, as a slight cough becomes more persistent or the horse is slow to pick up in condition; some never recover fully as a result of being pressed into full work too soon. This of course applies to all illnesses, some of which are more serious than others.

Coughs may be especially tiresome. One horse I knew originally picked up a cough at a show, and then had terrible bouts that kept him off work for weeks on end. He suffered considerably trying to breathe under these conditions.

Sweating

Following illness, it is important not to allow drastic changes in body temperature; this is another reason for not overworking the horse, causing him to sweat. Sweating is a natural process which removes excess bodyheat during exercise or infection. The horse's normal temperature is around 100.5°F (40.6°C).

Sometimes horses will sweat for reasons other than normal exertion. It may well be a clue to their internal anxieties, especially if they break out into a cold sweat after exercise; these tend to be worried animals which are not enjoying their work for whatever reason. They may simply be overworked, or more likely they are suffering stress from too much pressure; in other words they are being asked to do things beyond their capacity, whether this be physical or mental.

Rugging Up

Horses are often made miserable by over- or under-rugging. If they are under-rugged they will lose condition because they are too cold, left standing about in fields or in stables shivering off their weight. In their natural state they would move about and thus raise their circulation, but when confined to a small area this is not possible.

And although it is important to keep a horse warm when he is ill, it is sensible to use lightweight blankets rather than heavy ones which will make him feel weighed down. There are plenty of different types of rug to choose from, so this should not be a problem. If the horse

Clothing

I learned many years ago that horses do not much care for clothing! They may be grateful to be kept warm in winter, but in general they put up with the various garments they are made to wear with infinite long-suffering.

I also discovered to my cost that it is not just their clothing they object to but often ours as well. Squeaky riding boots or crackly macintoshes can give considerable alarm! My first dressage horse was horrified, I remember, the first time he felt the tails of my coat flapping on his back, and others I have had have disliked the feel of exercise sheets being blown by the wind. Anything unusual moving about on his back may cause alarm so introduce anything new with care.

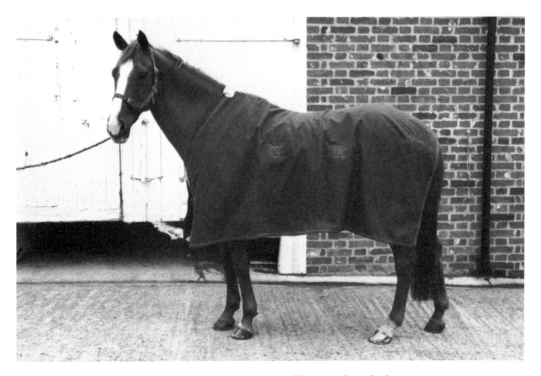

A New Zealand rug should be used to replace the stable rug when the horse is put out in the paddock for exercise.

Rugs that do not fit can be irritating and also may rub the horse, causing sores.

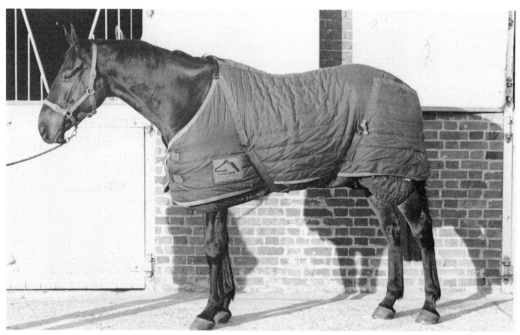

Cross-over straps help to prevent rugs from slipping when the horse lies down. This one looks comfortable for the horse.

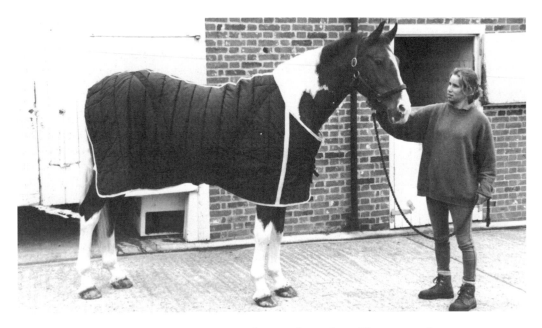

There are many different types of rug, some thinner than others. The type used will depend on whether the horse is clipped or what the weather is like.

Rugs can also be used to keep the coat clean and free from dust when the horse is stabled. Depending on the weather lighter or thicker rugs may be used.

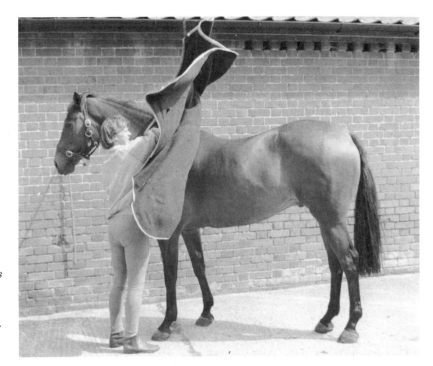

If a horse feels itchy he will often try to scratch himself while the rug is on. It can be very annoying for him not to be able to scratch properly, and this may start him rug tearing.

is sweating he should still be kept warm and only cooled off gradually.

In the winter a stable rug is necessary when the horse is in his loosebox; as the weather gets colder a blanket or two may be added. Some people use neck covers and hoods for extra protection. After work it is important that the animal is properly

cooled off and brushed over to remove sweat patches.

It may be necessary to use stable bandages for warmth or, in the case of an older horse, to give support. One of our horses had large windgalls which would disappear completely overnight as long as the bandages were put on after exercise. Windgalls in themselves are not really a handicap to a horse, although they are a consequence of strain or wear. Bandages should only be put on by those who know what they are doing, because if the tension on the tendons is too much or too little considerable damage can be done.

For the clipped horse, rugs replace the natural coat. It is especially important

Bandaging must be done with care. One that is not fixed adequately could cause a nasty accident.

Protection against injury when travelling is essential. This picture shows the bandages put on correctly with the padding drawn up over the knees.

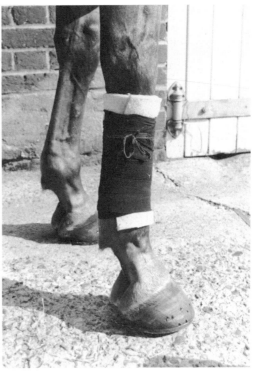

Some people like to use bandages when exercising for protection or support to the tendons. This must be done carefully and evenly and always with padding underneath the bandages. The bow should be on the outside as shown but the ends should be tucked in.

that they are put on if the horse is turned out, as he will have no natural oils or coat to prevent him getting cold. The fitting of New Zealand rugs is very important: so many horses become badly rubbed on their withers and shoulders or round their legs if the rug does not fit. Nor is it an acceptable practice to leave rugs on for long periods without checking on the horse's condition. We knew a horse which had been left in the same rug for months, and when it was eventually taken off the creature was covered in sheep ticks; imagine the misery it must have endured.

Skin Problems

Lice can be a problem in the winter months because they flourish in thick unclipped coats; the constant irritation they cause the horse drives him to incessant scratching.

Another most troublesome skin complaint is **sweet itch**, which affects the mane and tail. In spite of much research there is still as yet no cure, although the horse can be given relief by a variety of

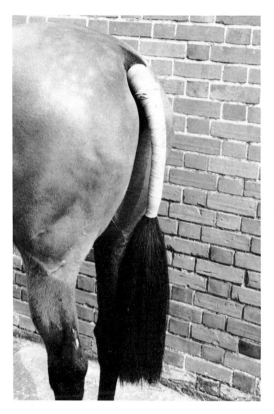

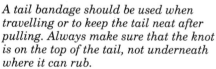

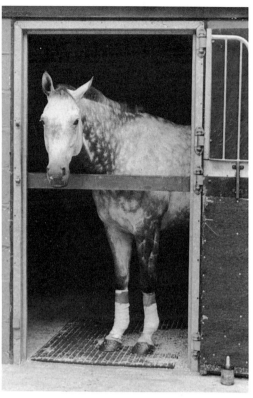

A tail bandage should be used when travelling or to keep the tail neat after pulling. Always make sure that the knot is on the top of the tail, not underneath where it can rub.

These bandages are odd which is incorrect and they do not appear to have any padding under them. It is quite a good idea to tape over them, as shown here, as in this case for greater security.

treatments. This should certainly be done so the horse does not have to suffer: if the condition is left untreated it eventually becomes very sore. When I was learning to jump I rode a pony with sweet itch, and the wretched animal could not bear its neck or withers to be touched. It did, however, teach me not to lean on the neck or hold the mane!

Ringworm is a highly contagious skin complaint and the tack, brushes and clothing belonging to the affected animal should be kept well away from others.

However, although it looks unpleasant, a horse does not otherwise appear to be distressed by it.

Clipping

A horse will almost certainly need clipping to some degree if he is to do much fast or continuous work, so that he does not sweat to excess. The clipping operation should be introduced with care and tact so as to minimize trauma for horse or owner. Run the clippers outside the stable first, so the horse can become used to the noise, and then introduce them to him slowly. The best place to begin clipping is at the shoulder so that you can reassure him by patting his neck and talking to him. Some horses always dislike being clipped; others do not mind at all. One of our mares was terrified of having her head done, but mainly I suspect because she associated it with having an ear twitched rather than from the actual clipping process.

> I cannot condone ear twitching. Quite apart from being very painful and possibly even damaging to the horse it can subsequently make him very difficult to bridle. If the twitch has to be resorted to at all, it should be applied to the upper lip, and it should be released at frequent intervals to allow the blood to circulate properly. This should only ever be undertaken by a professional, but preferably not at all.

Injuries

In dealing with any kind of injury it is wise to tie the horse up, or better still to have someone hold him, because many horses object to being handled when they are feeling hurt. They dislike the feel of water trickling down their legs while a wound is being cleaned, and most are frightened of an antiseptic puffer or spray at first. Thus it is important to try to avoid startling the horse by suddenly squirting something at it; if you do this to begin with, they may always be suspicious. Go about it quietly in the first place, however, and there should be no trouble in future.

> It is not just the horse which can get injured by being nervous: I remember having a rather nervous animal which, frightened by the smell of antiseptic, suddenly leaped in the air. But instead of jumping away from me, he unaccountably came towards me, landing on my foot which proceeded to swell at once and subsequently proved to be broken! Horses do, of course, suddenly take fright, and sometimes for no apparent reason; something nevertheless triggers off alarm signals, which is why we need to take great care in all our dealings with them.

Cracked heels are not exactly an injury, but they can nevertheless be very troublesome and can keep the horse off work. They are caused by the horse standing continuously in badly kept deep litter or in muddy fields, and it is not a condition to be ignored as some people seem to do. 'Only cracked heels', they say, as if it is nothing. But the horse is very likely to be in quite a lot of discomfort, as the skin may become very sore and swollen which can restrict movement. People will even punish a horse in this state 'for being unwilling' in his work: but why *should* he be willing when he is in such pain and discomfort?

Lameness

It is really quite amazing how surprised many owners are when their horse loses interest in his work because he is in pain. How often do we see lame horses being made to work regardless of their condition? Ignorance on the part of the owner is often the cause. I once had to tell a competitor that her horse was too lame to continue its dressage test, and she replied, 'Oh, he always goes like that!'. Owners and riders really should take more responsibility regarding the soundness of their horses. After all, we limp ourselves because we are in pain, so why should the horse be any different?

Having said that some horses do go unlevel due to stiffness or bridle lameness, but this is an entirely different matter (see Chapter 12).

Sores and Sarcoids

Horses will also lose interest in their work if they suffer from sarcoids growing in awkward places, such as under the belly, round the head or anywhere where the tack may rub them. Girth galls can be another problem, or a sore mouth. Owners must be prepared to treat these areas effectively or to rest the horse if necessary. A sore mouth must be particularly painful and is not going to make the horse feel co-operative.

Grooming is essential to good health but owners should use tact if the horse is specially sensitive.

There are some people who take a delight in deliberately injuring a horse's mouth, believing this will make it more responsive to the bridle. What a callous attitude! It is also a wholly misguided assumption, as the tissue round any injury becomes calloused once it is healed, and so becomes less sensitive, not more so.

Grooming

A horse grooms himself by rolling, though his intention is to keep necessary elements in his coat which will protect him from adverse weather. All the fussing and fiddling we humans get up to with our brushes and combs is therefore quite unnatural for him. Many horses dislike being groomed, especially the highly strung, thin-skinned, ticklish type. If you can imagine having your feet tickled or scratched while someone holds you down, you may be able to imagine how the horse feels when he is tied up and someone relentlessly attacks him with a hard brush!

Grooming is necessary in domesticity to

keep the horse clean and free from mud or sweat which might irritate him or cause sores. It can, however, be done with tact and with brushes which make allowance for the sensitivity of the horse's skin.

The Farrier

Keeping the feet in good condition is essential, so regular visits by the farrier are required. Some farriers are very good with horses; others can be rough and impatient. They have a job to do, so it is understandable if they become irritated by horses that will not pick up their feet or refuse to stand still. On the owner's part, time spent teaching a horse to co-operate while he is having his feet done is time well spent. It will help to avoid unpleasantness for the horse, and should prevent him developing a nervous attitude towards being shod. Youngsters are often frightened at first, and may need a good deal of reassurance. However, if they have had their feet attended to regularly from foalhood, they will soon learn to overcome any fears and waywardness.

The Vet

During his life the horse will probably need to see the vet several times for one reason or another, and this can be a very unnerving experience for him. Many of us don't much like going to hospital, and some people really dislike the smell. Horses are the same, and it is only fair to the horse and the vet to try and help the horse to remain calm. One girl groom I knew actually received the cortisone injection meant for the horse in her arm, because it was fidgeting about so much!

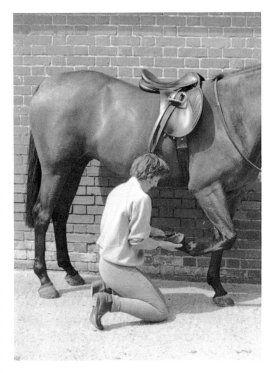

Feet must be kept in good condition and shoes constantly checked, but never kneel down beside the horse or pick up the feet in this way.

Man's Response

Whether the horse is healthy or ill, fat or thin, put yourself in his place and use common sense to guide you. When in doubt do not delay, enquire from the expert, whether it be the farrier or the vet, the feed merchant or the saddler. There is always someone out there who will know the answer. The main thing is not to let the horse suffer but to help him in every way possible. He will then think you are a great person and will really want to please you.

CHAPTER 9

The Horse's Mental Needs

As has already been mentioned, security is perhaps the most important factor contributing to the horse's mental health. It largely derives from a daily routine in which the horse knows what to expect and when; this means that not only should his food arrive at regular times, but he should be exercised at a similar time each day. His work should be planned in such a way that he knows what will be asked of him, and he should look forward to it and not dread it. In order that this feeling of security is created, the onus is on the owner to know and put such a routine into operation.

Stable Routine

Horse owners will undoubtedly have other commitments, either to work or to family or to both; for many people, horses are a hobby and as such have to be fitted in to their daily life. Because of this there can be no set rules regarding routine: everyone must adopt his own. This won't matter to the horse. What *would* matter would be if one day he got his breakfast at eight o'clock in the morning and the next not until twelve o'clock. In this circumstance he will feel restless or agitated and may well develop a stable vice as a result.

The horse needs to eat little and often, and the optimum is to give him at least four short feeds in every day. However, some owners simply cannot manage this, and in fact a horse will quite happily adapt his eating pattern to two feeds, one in the morning and one in the evening, if this is all that can be reasonably fitted in; I for one have never known horses to suffer any ill effects from this routine as compared to any other. Some of my business friends can only exercise their horses very early in the morning or after work at night. Again this does not matter to the horse, but it could be detrimental to his equanimity if he was used to a pattern which then became erratic.

A suitable routine might be as follows:

8.00 a.m. Check the horse over and straighten rugs, if any. Water and then give a short feed. Go and have your own breakfast. After breakfast muck out and give the horse a haynet. Tidy the yard.

10.00 a.m. Groom the horse and tack him up ready for exercise. Exercise for however long he needs, depending on what he is being trained for. Brush him over to make him comfortable, rug up.

12.30 p.m. Feed him, and leave him to eat his lunch. After lunch you may wish to exercise a second horse if you have one. Horses do get jealous, and this can be avoided if the horses can be done in the same order each day. Jealousy is not an emotion one would attribute to horses, but one mare we had made it quite plain how cross she was by putting her ears back and snapping and kicking out if her stable-mate was taken out in *her* normal exercise time!

The afternoon might also be a time to let the horse have an hour or two loose in the paddock, with a New Zealand rug if he is used to wearing stable rugs. After all the exercising and brushing off, tack can be cleaned and any other jobs attended to.

5.00 p.m.　Haynet, water and feed are given.

A fourth feed may be given later in the evening if required. Moreover, each time you enter the stable it is a good idea to pick up any droppings; this will make things more pleasant for the horse, besides which the next day's mucking out will be easier!

This routine assumes that you are a private horse owner with all the time in the world! However, perhaps if the above routine might be considered as the ideal, then individuals can vary the theme as required.

Many yards, such as a racing yard for example, would start much earlier in the day, and if there are a great many horses to do the timing is far tighter. And at a stud farm the whole routine may have to be adapted to allow for the covering of mares and so on – but each yard should stick to a system so that nothing is forgotten. Stallions in a yard can be disruptive when mares are in season, as the mares can make them agitated; also for those horses not involved in stud work it can create a disquieting atmosphere. These things have to be taken into account when planning how a yard should be run.

Exercise and Training Principles

To have a happy horse, two main points should be taken into account. First, the horse should, if possible, be exercised at a similar time each day as mentioned. The horse's 'internal clock' will tell him when to expect to be going out and if this does not happen or is erratic, he could become frustrated, upset or cross.

Secondly, the exercise he is given should be within his physical ability and explained clearly. It does not matter what job a horse is expected to do, the work entailed should be clear to him. Lessons need to be repeated until fully understood, and the horse given praise for his efforts.

As riders/handlers we can only teach the horse if we are absolutely certain ourselves of our objectives. Whatever the discipline involved, each person should find out what is needed to succeed and then discover how to do it. This will undoubtedly involve taking instruction from someone more knowledgeable, and then building on that knowledge. Also, those who want to learn can help themselves by watching others because something can be learned from almost everybody, even if it is only what *not* to do! Watching the experts will not only provide an insight into what is possible, but can also be a good incentive. All you need is an open mind!

Once you have decided on a goal, the next most vital factor is to begin at the beginning! You and the horse will need a sound base from which to develop together and from which gradual progress will be made. And don't expect too much too soon!

Learning about the horse's mind and the way he thinks is not a discovery which can be made in an instant: it takes years of patient study. Nevertheless he *does* think, even if in a limited capacity, and establishing a relationship is not simply a matter of forcing him to do what you want. An episode which demonstrated the horse's thought process was related to me recently by a knowledgeable friend. He had been giving his stallion some jumping lessons under saddle which the horse took to very happily. The following day he was put out to exercise in his usual paddock bordered by post and rail fencing. Normally he grazed out there quite peacefully, but on this particular morning he jumped from one paddock to another, evidently practising his new-found talent and happily investigating formerly unexplored territory!

On another occasion the same stallion was put in a different paddock while his own was being fertilized. This paddock led off the usual one, and was further from the yard. When the horse wanted to come in the only way he could attract attention was to bang on the gate with a forefoot, when someone would come and fetch him in. A week later when he was restored to his own paddock again he pushed open the gate between the two, stood on the far side and banged it with his foot until someone came to get him!

To my mind, these examples show clearly how horses are able to work things out. Many would argue that most

Most horses love to be turned out in a paddock to exercise, but there are some, however, who seem almost to prefer the security of their stable. They may like to go out and roll or have a gallop around but then they are ready to come in; I have known several of this sort who became quite frantic if not caught and restored to the safety of their loosebox. Thoroughbreds in particular seem to prefer to go out for only a short time. Perhaps being of such long-standing domestication their degree of natural instinct is less than other types. At any rate, I have never found it beneficial to leave a horse in a field if he does not want to be there.

instances attributed to an apparent thought process were actually only the result of chance discovery. Undoubtedly this is true, but equally it is not the only reason, I am sure.

Daily Training Routine

Many horse owners will have competitions as their goal, and if they are ambitious, the route to achieving that goal should be carefully thought out. Unless an owner has a clearly structured training programme for the horse, he is not likely ever to reach his aim.

At home a training routine will therefore be mapped out and the horse taught what is required. Each day he should be brought to his schooling area and first loosened up for the real work ahead. If the horse is ridden he should warm up in a relaxed way before being brought more firmly onto the aids. This may take five to ten minutes depending on the age and ability of the horse.

Once his muscles are thoroughly warm, his body will be able to respond to his mind in an effective way. He is now in a position of receptiveness to the demands of his rider and the planned lesson should begin.

Individuals will vary enormously in their capacity to grasp the question being asked. Generally, the younger the animal the quicker it is, as it has no previous questions to unravel. Older horses may have had several owners, all of whom will have asked their questions in a different way. Also the musculature of those horses will have developed more which can be a disadvantage if they have not been developed in the right way. It is therefore usually much harder to re-train an older horse than it is to train a young one, and much harder for the older horse to sort out in his mind.

During the lesson the horse should have several rests, and an ideal moment is following an improvement or an obvious moment of comprehension. Then he should be allowed to walk in a relaxed way and given the chance to stretch. This is a reward in itself but can be accompanied by praise. Titbits, however, should *not* be given at this point, as the horse may learn to expect them. A friend's horse being rewarded in this way soon developed the habit of stopping dead to receive its sugar each time she came to walk! Eventually she had to smack him for this, which was muddling and made him quite resentful.

During a lesson the horse will need several 'rests' to relax his muscles and have time to take in what he has been learning.

It is very important for the horse's mental stability that when training him, a lesson is always ended on a high note and begun again the following day at the same point. Obvious progress is made in this way, much of which is probably due to the horse's remarkable memory, but also because he does seem to think about what he has learnt overnight.

The trainer should also bear in mind that the horse will remember the tiniest improvement as long as he is rewarded. In fact for best results each training session should be based on a simple lesson which should be repeated until the horse has grasped it thoroughly. Only then move to the next. So much of a horse's unwillingness or lack of cooperation is because he has had too many questions thrown at him in a jumbled way. Not only can he physically not respond because his brain has not had time to unravel all the instructions fired at him, but he is confused as to which one to try to answer. Consistency is also very important.

Thus a lesson must not contain too many questions, at least while the horse is learning. An older horse that knows his work may go through a varied routine of different exercises without getting confused – but confusion should be avoided at all costs, as this leads to all kinds of problems (see Chapter 12).

The length of a lesson may vary a good deal, but as a general rule approximately three-quarters of an hour is sufficient. A cooling off period after the lesson is important to allow the horse to relax his muscles before being put back into his stable. Also during those moments he will have the chance to become calm in his mind. This will help him to avoid tensions and prevent him breaking out once he is back in his loosebox.

The Rein-Back

This exercise can cause problems! I remember in particular a mare we were training who positively panicked at being asked to go backwards, so much so that she would launch forwards and try to gallop off! Some time later we were investigating her past and discovered that at one time she used to go backwards as an evasion and had been beaten for it by a previous owner!

I have known quite a number of horses who have discovered that by standing in a hollow outline with their hind legs out behind them they can avoid reining back. In this position it is virtually impossible, which is why it is important to have a balanced and square halt before attempting the exercise.

Shows

Because of the goals that owners set themselves the horse must be taken out to shows to further his education. However, this experience can be most unnerving for him. In the first place he may have to undergo all manner of strange preparations such as having his mane and tail pulled or plaited, being bathed, and almost certainly wearing bandages and a rug or a sheet. He may be expected to wear different tack to that which he is normally trained in. He will have to go into a lorry, and perhaps worst of all, he will be leaving his friends and his familiar surroundings. It is this last element which can cause a lot of stress.

If possible before taking the horse anywhere new, try to create a similar atmosphere by bringing in other horses for company, or putting some of the probable hazards around the schooling area. Flowers in pots, flags, plastic bags, music playing or other horses galloping past should all be part of the preparations.

If a horse lives on his own he will very likely become tremendously excited at the sight of others of his species, and this may well prevent him from being able to concentrate; as a result he will completely forget all those lessons learned at home. Thus he will need to spend some time looking around at all the sights, many of which may be new to him.

If he is over-excited it will be pointless trying to make him work properly until he has settled down. Sometimes a while on the lunge will help him to burn off excess energy and make him calm enough to think what he is being asked to do. Nor will a horse work properly if he becomes overtired. Under show conditions it is very difficult to assess how long you will need to ride in; only trial and error will produce an answer.

Some horses rely particularly on others for their security, and will fret unless they have a stable companion; at a show they may well feel lost if their friend is left at home. Many will spend their time calling to see if they get a response, and failing the answer they hope for, may then 'hang' to another horse or to their lorry for the security they crave.

It may be difficult to persuade a horse to leave the box park and to go into the next field where the ring is. This is because he knows only too well where his own lorry is, with its familiar smell, and he doesn't want to leave it. One of our horses once took fright at the unexpected sight of a man selling balloons, and bolted with my daughter right across the showground, back into the box park and up the ramp of the lorry before it would stop!

> Calling out to other horses can be a wretched nuisance, as I found to my cost at one dressage competition where my gelding neighed throughout the test to the mare who was left in the trailer. She, I might add, took no notice whatsoever, and remained calmly eating her hay! That particular gelding had formerly had a very insecure life with several unsympathetic owners, and was, I am sure, yelling to his pal hoping for reassurance.

Another problem arising from going to shows is that it breaks the normal, everyday routine. This can be as traumatic for the humans as it is for the horses, causing a variety of nervous reactions. It is worth remembering that any change in our own behaviour is felt and registered by the horse, thus causing him to wonder and possibly react differently himself.

Any change in the feeding pattern may cause upset. The horse may well go off his food for the day due to excitement, and he may as a result start to look quite tucked up. His digestion can be affected adversely. If at all possible, stick to your normal routine with adjusted size of feeds; and beware that a greedy horse doesn't fill himself up too much, because he may then not be able to do the work required of him.

Signals

Sighing

A horse's sigh is very similar in meaning to our own, and certainly seems to be used at times of resignation or boredom. If the trainer/handler notes the situation that causes the horse to sigh most he may be able to see whether it was induced by some form of unpleasantness which in the future can be avoided.

Coughing and Sneezing

Some people are of the opinion that apart from the obvious respiratory reasons that cause a horse to cough, there are also occasions when he appears to do so deliberately to get out of work. I have found that on the whole this theory is false. When a horse coughs he does so because he needs to, not because he plans to avoid his work. If, on the other hand, he discovers that when he coughs he is allowed to walk about on a loose rein or is taken back to the stable, after a while this will register in his mind and he could learn by association that it might be used as an excuse. Exactly the same can be said of sneezing: if the horse discovers that by sneezing he can gain a loose rein he will soon use this to his own advantage.

Some horses which suffer from stress do use sneezing as a form of relief. Given reassurance they will usually stop.

Man's Response

In order to provide the horse with a secure home in which he feels safe and will therefore relax and be able to use his brain effectively, we must do our best to follow a regular pattern. We must take into account all the moments when, to the horse, there is a change, however small. Man should love his animal, not sentimentally to the point of spoiling it, but with care and anticipating its needs. He should give it confidence from his handling of it so that it will be persuaded to give its trust and be rewarded for it. He should provide a calm and peaceful atmosphere both in the stable and out of it so that his horse can enjoy security and peace of mind.

CHAPTER 10

Evasions and Complexes

Catching

'First catch your horse' is an obvious maxim but very true: he has to be approached in such a way that he will allow himself to be caught. If he is stabled one might suppose that catching him would be an easy job, but this is not so – I have spent many hours sitting in the straw trying to gain the trust of a wild and untouched youngster which refuses to come up to me. It is a most frustrating business and requires endless patience to be successful.

Those who breed their own stock generally ensure that foals are accustomed to being handled early in their lives, providing the mothers can be caught! Once a foal discovers that humans are not frightening it will in fact quickly become cheeky and then has to be put in its place. Unfortunately many foals do not have a good start because they are left unhandled for too long, and by the time it becomes

Many horses are difficult to catch. If the horse enjoys his work and is attached to his owner he will be more keen to come. A titbit or some nuts in a bucket usually do the trick.

essential to catch them they are big and strong and far harder to catch and control. Sadly, as soon as a 'round up' becomes necessary a youngster experiences fear, and once fear is present his immediate reaction will be to run away, or to bite or kick if touched.

Wild animals do not respond to the human voice or to titbits until some time after they have become accustomed to being handled, but once they have reached this stage the voice is invaluable, as in fact is the titbit. Most horses cannot resist food, so once a preference is discovered it can be a great help in catching them – and

Having caught one horse, always be careful that the others left in the field do not try to come as well.

A bucket containing some 'feed' can save a lot of time when trying to catch the horse.

horses do undoubtedly express preferences: some will not touch sugar but love a carrot or an apple, while others will reject these but will fall over themselves to get to a Polo mint!

A bucket with a few horse nuts in the bottom that rattle enticingly as you approach will catch almost anything. With a particularly difficult horse try placing the nose of the headcollar in the bucket so that once his head is in it you only have to position the headpiece. This is unlikely to work with those crafty ones who have learned how not to be caught, however, as they know perfectly well that the headcollar is there. A more stealthy approach with a rope hidden behind your back is needed for these.

Although a patient approach is best, some animals do have to be cornered in order to catch them; nevertheless it is these occasions that tend to provoke in them a 'catching' complex. It does not really take much imagination to appreciate that if an animal has an unpleasant experience of any kind he is less likely to want to be caught. Similarly a horse that swings away when he is being bridled has obviously had a bad start; those that don't mind have been handled sensibly and sympathetically right from the beginning.

Ponies that live out are often rather naughty about being caught, but one can imagine that the freedom of the field is far more attractive to them than being made to tear about at the whim of their young owners. Food will generally attract these, however.

Because horses respond to the human voice once they know and understand it, it can be a great help in catching those who are reluctant. 'Free lungeing' may also be effective in this respect: making the horse trot in circles round you whilst you 'control' him with the words of command he knows; after a while he generally becomes rather bored and on command will come to walk and then halt and so allow itself to be caught.

Trying to catch a really frightened horse can be dangerous to both horse and human. If he 'runs blind' in fear he may go over or through anyone or anything in his way and it may not be possible to catch him in this state; and it goes without saying that it is very important never to do anything that could bring a horse to this pitch of anxiety. The best policy with this type of horse is to persuade him to follow another horse into a stable or barn where it is easier to establish contact and gain his trust.

Leading

An animal will at some point have to learn to lead. Foals are taught to wear a foal slip although they are not actually led by it to start with; the rope is placed around their neck, and the person leading holds it with the left hand. The right hand is then placed round the foal's hindquarters to help encourage it forwards. If someone else leads the mare in front, the foal is usually persuaded to follow quietly. If you try to lead a foal as you would an older horse, the foal's natural instinct is to pull against whatever is restraining it. It may then learn that in a battle of strength it can win, or it may slip up in the effort of pulling back. Either way it is a bad lesson for the foal and an experience which may result in further leading problems.

Once an animal has found that it is stronger than its owner there will be trouble. We once owned a mare who could not be led in a headcollar as she knew she could get away. When leading her to the field we had to unclip the rope in the stable and just slip it through the ring on the headcollar; then as soon as she pulled away the rope would slip easily through the ring. The field gate had to be already open, or I believe she would have crashed through it. We had tried holding her by various methods but she was very strong and it was not worth the hassle. In every other way she was entirely docile!

Young horses must be taught to be mannerly when they are turned loose in a paddock. They should always be taken through the gate, turned back to face it,

It is most important that a 'foal slip' is introduced to the young animal early on so that he may learn to lead as soon as possible.

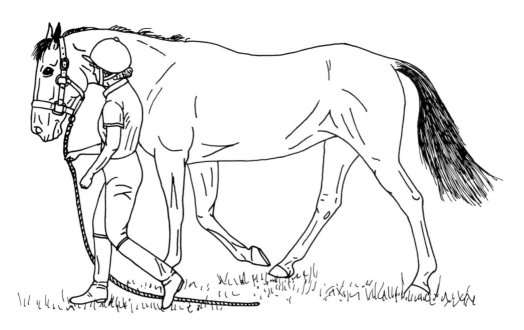

For safety reasons always make sure that the end of the rope is held up off the ground.

and only then be released. If this practice is followed the problem of rushing and pulling away should never arise.

It is general practice to lead horses from the near side and it is from the near side that much of our handling and tacking up is done. However, it is important that as much training as possible is done on both sides of the horse to avoid unnecessary nervousness. Many people are surprised at how nervous their horse becomes when suddenly they do something, or lead him from the off side for some reason.

Tying Up

A common problem is for a horse to object to being tied up; many will pull back and break the rope or hurt themselves in the process. I nearly lost a very good horse once by tying it to a five-barred gate while I inspected its feet. Out of the blue it panicked and pulled back so sharply that the gate came off its hinges, and away went the horse down the road with the gate in tow. It went several hundred yards before I could catch it. Miraculously it was not hurt at all, although I had imagined every leg would be broken! This particular horse had a phobia about being tied, and obviously found it unacceptably restrictive; she would even pull back inside a lorry. Once loose she would stand as quiet as a lamb, but I was never able to cure her and we both learned to live with it!

Learning to tie up is important, however, and something that should be taught quite early in a foal's life. On the Continent foals are tied to their mothers'

Owners should be aware that when tied the horse may decide to break free. Many disasters result from this happening.

Give a good deal of thought as to where to tie up safely. Also be aware of the horse catching the rope in his teeth or chewing it to pieces while you are not looking.

Horses, especially young ones, should never be left tied up without supervision.

Although this is a safer method, the foal soon learns that it can break away from the restriction and a bad habit is formed.

When travelling horses I would, however, advocate that the rope is attached to string and not directly to the ring. I once travelled two horses in a trailer, one of which panicked, frightening the other. Both fell down so that their legs were pinned under the partition. Their halter ropes were attached directly to the rings and were pulled so tight as to be impossible to loosen, even though slip knots had been used. The difficulty we had in removing the partition so we could manoeuvre the horses into a position to remove the headcollars was unbelievable. After that we always tied up to string attached to the rings and never went anywhere without a penknife!

Remember that leather headcollars will break if enough pressure is put on them; the nylon headcollars mostly used today will not, and can cause severe 'burning'.

rollers and in this way learn to be controlled; to them this is an acceptable restriction.

In this country a well known Welsh section D stud teaches all its foals to tie to a ring by attaching a chain to the foal slip from a few days old. The mare is tied also, and although the foal will have a short fight it soon accepts the situation and I understand they have never had any accidents. This method may well be more suitable than the more tentative approach of tying up to a piece of string attached to the ring which breaks in an emergency.

Lungeing

Lungeing is the first step towards further education and should be the basis of the rapport between horse and man. It is most important that confidence and trust are developed at this stage: done well, the horse will be well set up for the future.

The unskilled can get into a lot of trouble trying to lunge. This trainer has dressed her horse correctly and has placed herself in a good position to control him.

Having lunge lessons to improve position is very useful if it is done on a safe schoolmaster. A lungeing whip should be carried by the trainer to aid control over the horse.

Sadly this is often the very moment when the opposite happens!

Lungeing is not simply a matter of putting a horse on the end of a rope and chasing him round in a circle with the whip; it is a skilled job that requires study and practice (see Chapter 12). Many owners do not properly understand how to lunge and as a result cause all sorts of problems, one of the first being that they let the horse go. This can happen only too easily if you are caught in a vulnerable position where the horse can take the advantage, that is directly behind or in front of you. Also if you have forgotten to put your gloves on and the lunge rein whips through your hands giving a painful 'burn'; or if you have forgotten to take off your spurs and one gets caught to the other immobilizing you! Yes, we have all been through it!

If the horse does become loose with a lunge rein trailing he will certainly frighten himself, he may tangle himself in it or may become attached to some object. Whatever happens it is highly dangerous and can cause serious problems in the future.

Some horses are also very artful. A stallion we had to break in had learned that to get out of doing what we wanted, all he had to do was to rear up and put a foreleg over the lunge line – and however quick we were, he was quicker! As an answer to this we attached two lunge reins, one on each side of the cavesson. Undaunted, this

A correctly attired horse and trainer, although the trainer should have a lungeing whip in order to long-rein the horse correctly.

A loose lunge rein is highly dangerous and a situation such as this may well leave the horse with permanent mental difficulties.

clever fellow reared up and put one leg over one side and the other leg over the other side! This happened repeatedly until we were obliged to find an alternative way of handling him; this was to drive him, having first brought the reins back through rings on top of a roller. Disappointed that his trick wouldn't work in this circumstance, the stallion gave in and actually learned his lessons.

Tacking Up

Many problems derive from this point in the horse's life. Youngsters can be irrevocably put off by having a bit clanked unsympathetically against their teeth or leatherwork dragged over their ears. Bad bridling experiences early on can lead to great difficulties later. Some horses learn to clamp their mouths shut to avoid taking the bit; others will back away or try to bite or even rear to prevent a bridle from being put on. This can take weeks to overcome and may always be a problem.

Putting on a saddle properly is just as important. If it is placed carefully on the horse's back he will not resent it, but if it is banged against his withers or slapped down on his back, he may well show his dislike by attempting to bite or kick.

Doing up the girth can produce quite a few problems, too. I have a friend who rides her horse with such a slack girth as to be dangerous in my opinion, but the horse in question had problems with rollering when he was started and as a result cannot stand a tight girth. However, if initially he had been

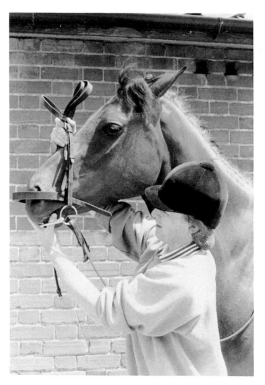

The correct way to put on a bridle. Note the thumb of the rider's left hand, which is pressing between the horse's lips in order to get him to open his mouth. Many bridling problems arise from trying to force the bit against the teeth.

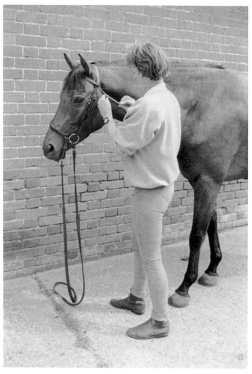

Clearly this rider is at fault: reins should never be left dangling.

persuaded to accept the roller calmly when he was broken and was then saddled correctly, it would not now be a problem.

Another horse would allow the girth to be done up without fuss but would then 'blow himself out', and feeling it tight he would panic, rearing or bucking to get rid of it. If you were in the saddle at the time this was not pleasant! We overcame this by using a girth with an elastic insert by the buckles; because it had some 'give' in it, it avoided the feeling of absolute restriction that caused the problem.

We also had a pony that would only tolerate the girth being done up if it was done just one hole at a time; if at any time he felt too restricted he would throw himself over backwards. If you proceeded slowly until it was tight enough he accepted it without fuss.

All horses have their quirks and complexes. Rather than try to fight them it is often better to analyse *why* they object so strongly, and to proceed in the best way possible by accommodating them.

The first time that the horse has boots or bandages put on his legs he may well feel worried. Some do not like them at all, and will travel perfectly well without bandages but really badly with them.

Try to be tactful when putting on the saddle, the horse may display his annoyance at any lack of sympathy by trying to bite or kick.

Every owner has to find out what worries his horse and either train him to accept it, or give in for the sake of peace and quiet! As long as the latter course of action is not likely to cause any danger, this is sometimes the best policy.

Mounting

Some horses do have a complex about being mounted. A very well known show stallion had to leave the ring because he would not stand for the judge to mount him. This can be embarrassing, not to say annoying, especially if you have been called in at the top of the line!

Mounting problems no doubt originate from a horse's very first experiences of having a rider on his back. If the job is

done carefully, allowing the horse time to feel and become accustomed to the rider's weight gradually, he will not dread the process. If, on the other hand, it is done roughly or the rider drags the saddle to the side, the horse will soon associate the mounting procedure with pain.

It amazes me how often the horse is blamed for not standing still when the rider has just dug his toe into the horse's ribs or has nearly pulled the horse over pulling himself up into the saddle! He then sits down with a thump on the horse's back and wonders why it nearly collapses underneath him! These riders are clearly unsympathetic and quite lacking in common sense too, or they would work out for themselves why the horse is unhappy and dances about trying to resist them mounting at all!

I find it incomprehensible why so many riders refuse to use a mounting block; it is far easier for the person mounting and much better for the horse. Every horse should be taught to stand still when being mounted, so it is a good policy to take a little longer over it in the first place, teaching him to wait until *you* are ready to move off. This strategy will make him sensible and safer. The mounting block should be situated in a safe position where the horse cannot subsequently fall over it. Once the horse accepts being mounted from a block in this way he will not mind being mounted from the ground should the occasion arise.

Loading

It is not in the least surprising that many horses do not wish to go into their lorries or trailers. Many owners evidently have no idea how to drive a horse in order to

It is common sense to place the trailer in an inviting position, which may help to encourage the horse to board. Leaving the front ramps down gives maximum light. In addition, the partition could be swung to give extra room while the horse is being loaded.

When the horse is in the trailer never tie him until the back ramp is up. This avoids pulling back and, possibly, broken fingers.

give him a comfortable journey, and if he feels unsafe or loses his feet he is not going to want to cooperate. For example, the speed with which some drivers negotiate a roundabout is astonishing. They must be able to hear their horse clattering about in the back trying to keep his feet, but they continue regardless. And animals are often seen at shows with injuries sustained on the journey – though by anybody's book it is rather foolish to lame the horse or miss a class on account of thoughtless driving. Nor does the problem end there, however, because those animals that are constantly driven without due consideration will, in time, refuse to load willingly.

A horse can be forced into a box or trailer by various means, but this is not really the answer, and some do feel genuinely nervous of the small space they are being asked to travel in. This I feel is entirely reasonable. For example, I once owned a big Thoroughbred who travelled perfectly given a whole trailer but obviously felt too restricted when partitioned. Going into a trailer even without the

This lorry has a nice low ramp which horses like, but it has been positioned near to a concrete drive which can be very slippery especially if the horse is reluctant to go in.

partition was a worry to him, and he would stand at the bottom of the ramp trying to pluck up the courage to enter. When he did it was in a great rush, but we had to let him tackle it in this way otherwise he felt he could not manage it. It was the same procedure coming out, but providing we all stood clear he unloaded himself quite adequately.

Another horse we owned was just the opposite and travelled much more happily if he was wedged quite tightly into a partition, obviously gaining confidence from the secure feeling.

Reluctance to load is quite often the result of a badly positioned vehicle. If the approach to the ramp is from a tight turn or there is too much space around it, the horse will choose to go anywhere but up it!

A steep ramp, too, is very off-putting, especially if the horse once slips up; he will then be genuinely nervous.

If it is possible to park out of the sight of others the horse will be less distressed and more inclined to oblige. Also, an older, more experienced horse travelled with the

Owners with trailers are often surprisingly reluctant to swing a partition over so that their horse has more space to get in. Whether this is laziness or lack of forethought, it could well cause them to spend hours trying to persuade their horse to go in when he might have found the extra space more acceptable and walked up happily.

When unloading do not invite accidents by having other animals, children or tack on, or near, the ramp.

nervous individual will be an encouragement and may help him to overcome any fears.

The Headshy Horse

This problem is often caused in the course of trying to load a horse into a vehicle or when leading him in and out of the stable. Pain normally causes a horse to fling up his head, so once a horse has hit his head on something he will often do it again simply because he anticipates the pain but is not able to rationalize what caused it. Moreover if pain is associated with a

specific situation, the problem is likely to recur.

A typical example of this was a big mare that we once owned; she was being led into her loosebox one day when something startled her and she flung up her head and hit it on top of the doorway. From that day on, every time she went in or out of the stable she flung her head up and hit it again; and needless to say after a while she refused to go into the stable at all. We did persuade her to go in eventually by reversing her into it, but it was distressing for her and for us. Eventually she was sold to someone who kept her in a barn!

This story only goes to show how easily horses can develop a complex and how tiresome the outcome can be.

Lying Down

It is most important for all creatures to have moments of rest when they can relax completely and revitalize their energies. Horses normally lie down in their stable or paddock at least once during a twenty-four hour period, and foals and young animals will need to do so even more often.

Some horses lie down quite a lot, others not at all, the latter generally being horses that are too worried or lacking in trust in their owners to do so. This does not say much for the owner, who has evidently failed to generate that feeling of security which the horse derives from his stable and exercise routine. Also, if he is stabled there should be adequate space for him to get up and down.

Nor will a horse lie down if he feels vulnerable, which sometimes happens if horses are able to see each other through or over a partition wall: one threatening another in any way may make it feel too

If the horse starts to 'nap', do not instantly blame him. There is probably a very good reason which the owner may have caused.

nervous to take a proper rest. Although this is not exactly a complex, it can become one if allowed to go on for too long.

Napping

How often do we hear people say, 'That horse was born nappy!' Certainly it sometimes appears that way, but I personally do not believe it. My experiences with many exceedingly nappy horses have indicated that all their problems can be traced back to the way they have been handled. Naturally there are some horses which in temperament are inherently much less willing than others, and these are the ones which are most likely to resent the questions asked of them.

Napping has the potential to start very early in a horse's life. Even a foal will try out his strength, and if he triumphs over his handler this experience is remembered

for ever. Horses, even the most stupid, are nevertheless very quick to discover ways of avoiding our demands, and they never forget how to do it. Even years later they will, given the opportunity, recall an incident when they came out 'on top'.

Otto was a fine example. He was very nappy and had had many owners all of whom he had found a way of removing from the saddle. Not one could quite recall exactly how he did it, but they all found themselves sitting on the ground. He had in fact learned every trick in the book,

---

My riding master used to say, 'Whatever the horse wants to do, do the opposite!' Not bad advice if you think about it. We all want the horse to do what we want, but if we let him have his own way we may never achieve ours.

---

from swinging round to galloping side-ways, refusing to move, to lying down! Being pre-warned and therefore extra cautious I managed to stay on his back for the next seven years, by which time he had become an Advanced dressage horse and therefore, I hoped, tractable to my whims.

One morning I was riding in a strange school surrounded by a hedge. Quite suddenly a bird flew out of it, Otto swung round and I feebly fell off. I remounted and carried on, but the very next day in the same school and on reaching the point where I had fallen off, Otto tried to swing round to remove me again! In spite of all the training we had been through together he had never forgotten how to capitalize on an evasion!

Man's Response

If we can accept that *we* actually cause our horses to think up ways to avoid doing what we want them to do, perhaps in future we will think more sensibly before we act. Often because we do not realize we are making mistakes we find ourselves landed with a problem; yet if we would only take the time to learn about our horses, by thinking and planning we could avoid those situations.

Our horses are very often quicker than we are and remember much better than we do. So before we lay blame at their door, perhaps we should try to work out whether it should not more fairly be laid at ours!

Flies

Many horses are neurotic about flies and really hate them buzzing round, especially if they are the hornet variety that look like bees and have a long curling tail. Some horses will gallop about frantically trying to escape their persistent and annoying attentions. Their anxiety is perfectly reasonable, because if these creatures settle they can inflict a serious sting.

Horse flies are extremely irritating as they actually suck blood and can cause painful or itchy swelling as well, and most horses are unable to concentrate on their work if horse flies settle on their skin. When riding, it is usually necessary to swat them quickly, and although this may startle the horse at first, he will soon learn to associate the action with relief.

Ordinary flies are also very tiresome and will swarm round any part of the horse's body, but in particular the eyes and muzzle. Horses have their own method of dealing with them, which is to shake the head or swish the tail, and in cases of extreme aggravation the animal will rub itself on a tree or fence. Even these ordinary flies can cause the horse a great deal of trauma if his skin is especially sensitive, although how much can only be determined by each horse's reaction to the problem because just as humans vary in skin sensitivity, so do animals. Hair density also plays a part, and those animals with thinner or clipped coats might be more susceptible.

If the aggravation caused by flies is too much for the horse to cope with by itself, there are various products which can be used as a repellent. Fly fringes or anti-fly discs are also useful on headcollars when horses are turned out in the summer, or discs can be attached to bridles, although they may not be allowed in some competitions.

It is important to understand that horses will want to rid themselves of anything that is annoying them in their own way, and if not allowed to do so, they may become quite frantic. In this state they can become awkward or even temporarily unmanageable, so we must do what we can to help.

CHAPTER 11

The Horse on the Ground

Many situations can cause horses to become upset, and when they do they often behave in an irrational manner. Whenever this happens it is up to us to work out the reason.

The horse's mind is governed by many fears: of being trapped in a tight place; of being separated from his friends or his familiar surroundings; of being hurt by some object; or being forced to take part in some activity beyond his capabilities. These fears quite often lead him into relatively dangerous situations so he actually ends up in a much worse position than he would have done had he not panicked in the first place.

The horse's generally nervous nature can be attributed to inborn fearfulness, whereas most of the fears he has in his domestic state have evolved from some specific occurrence. Because of his superior hearing, sight and smell he often senses things before we do, reacting with tension or anxiety. I have heard it said that a horse picks up many vibrations from the ground which are transmitted as warnings to the brain, and this would certainly account for some of his apparently odd reactions. This 'early warning' system would undoubtedly have been invaluable to him in the wild, and has no doubt been retained through evolution.

Many of a horse's strange habits I am sure are derived from boredom or irritation; they are often discovered by accident but he continues to indulge in them for something to do. He can remember incidents from way back in his life, and in fact is able to recall the minutest detail. Thus mentally he is often exceedingly able; physically, however, he is frequently awkward and ungainly, and even when loose in the field will gallop about in such a way that he slips and falls over. By his own actions the horse often puts himself in a potentially dangerous situation.

To appreciate his mental state at any one time we have to take each incident in context.

Claustrophobia

One area in which a horse can feel most claustrophobic is when he is travelling. Although his natural state is to be free-ranging, domestication has thoroughly accustomed him to a restricted environment; it therefore seems strange that he would suddenly develop a phobia against being put into a horsebox or trailer – yet this happens.

Initially the experience for him can be alarming, having to negotiate a ramp and going from light into dark. He may find the ramp awkward and slippery and the darkness unnerving, and no animal is willing to go anywhere unless it can see what it is going towards, in case there is danger involved.

Once the horse arrives inside the vehicle he will soon discover that he is trapped there. A placid animal may not worry about this at all, but a more highly strung one can find it very alarming, and even more so when the vehicle starts to move. Mental alarm will soon turn into physical tension, and this in itself often causes the problems. Finding itself so restricted, the horse may start to struggle and this usually results in it being unable to balance. When it finds itself slipping about, its brain ceases to function rationally, and the messages from brain to limb become distorted and confused.

After this has happened, injuries may well follow, and this development only serves to exacerbate the situation as the horse is unable to work out for himself how to stop the pain he is causing himself.

Some horses end up frightened from the experience, others become more and more cross. I had one like this which in fact was not a bad traveller at all. He would load perfectly well and would stand absolutely still for two hours; but if the journey was longer than that he would start to buck, and he would continue to buck for the rest of the trip. When this first happened I thought he must be having some kind of seizure, but having travelled in the back of the vehicle with him I could see that he wasn't alarmed, simply cross. No doubt he had had enough of being squashed into a small space and just wanted to get out.

Of course horses suffer from claustrophobia in places other than in vehicles, although this is much less common. Some dislike being confined in a stable and will constantly kick out or rush round trying to get out. If taken out and put in a paddock they instantly become calm.

Each instance of claustrophobia has to be dealt with separately. Our bad travellers have all been quite settled given more space, and the hysterical stabled ones have become much calmer if put next door to another horse they could see. However, in my experience some horses do actually suffer from travel sickness, and this of course has a lot to do with their dislike of going on a journey. Because it is physically impossible for a horse actually to be sick, he shows his misery by a general attitude of depression; and I did once have a horse hardly able to stand after a sea crossing.

Panic

A horse that feels panicky often betrays his state by frequently passing faeces or even having diarrhoea, sometimes so severe that the underside of the tail becomes sore. If this happens on a journey when he is wearing a tail bandage the soreness can become acute. A panicking horse will also show great tension throughout his body and his eyes will be wide open, possibly showing the whites. His ears will flick nervously to and fro and he will be very restless. He may even step on his own feet in his agitation.

A horse in this state does not think clearly. He is so worked up that he may do all sorts of foolish things, such as jumping some unlikely object or pushing through a barbed-wire fence.

Panic is often caused because one horse is taken away from another. A very good horse we had once jumped a five-barred gate onto a passing car because someone unwittingly took his friend away. Another managed to jump the breast bar of a trailer, ending up upside down on the front ramp and still tied up, because his friend had vanished from sight!

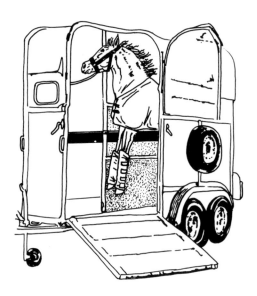

Owners should be constantly aware that some horses will go to any lengths to follow their friends.

Getting Cast

Horses love to roll, and need to do so for the reasons already explained earlier in this book. If they do so when stabled there is always a chance that they may become cast. A horse is not able to work out that if he rolls over as he would in a field then he is going to arrive at a solid wall, ending up in a position where he cannot move.

Once in that position he may struggle, and by kicking himself off the wall get himself up. More often than not, however, he will be stuck. Placid horses will generally then lie where they are and wait to be rescued, but the more nervous ones often thrash about in a panic.

I had one chestnut mare that regularly became cast every night even with an anti-cast roller, and she was so accustomed to finding herself in this position that she would wait, patiently tapping gently on the wall, until we came to extricate her. She was obviously not unhappy with this situation although *we* were soon fed up with our lack of sleep! We tried her in a larger stable but this did not help at all, and she was eventually removed to a much smaller stable where she still lay down but never tried to roll!

It can't be right to pull a horse's tail to get him away from a wall because it is so easily damaged; nor should the head be pulled into an unnatural position. It is

A horse in a panic will jump the wheelbarrow left in the stable doorway or even jump the door itself if he is that desperate to reach his pals.

One youngster being weaned from its mother managed to break a window six feet from the ground with its front feet in an attempt to regain her company. I also knew of one horse that frequently bit itself in a frenzy because it became so panicked at the loss of its companion.

Separating horses intentionally for some reason such as weaning, or merely because you want to take one for a ride without the other, can cause problems.

To overcome these moments of panic we must plan our strategy carefully, being aware of what might cause the panic in the first place. It is not always easy to anticipate, but it is important if we are to save ourselves from a nervous breakdown and our horses from worry and injury.

> Horses that worry when cast I am sure do so because in that moment they feel extremely vulnerable. Once they understand that they are being helped their panic may subside, but because we cannot explain to them what is happening it is difficult for them to remain calm.

A horse that is cast may well panic as his instinctive ability to protect himself is prevented.

usually best to help the horse by placing – not tying – ropes or straps around his feet nearest the wall and then pulling him over and away from it. He will then be able to get up to his feet. It is important to stand clear as he gets up, as he may still be in rather a state. Also help him to relax again by using the voice soothingly.

Bullying

This can occur in two ways: those animals that bully each other, and those who bully humans. The ones that bully each other generally do so on account of food. Horses spend a considerable proportion of their lives thinking about food: in the wild they must find it for themselves and their instincts lead them to it; when domesticated they rely on others to provide it, and they desire it at very regular intervals or preferably all the time. When it is restricted or limited, either agitation or anger will result: highly strung horses will become agitated, and the rest may become cross. All are potential bullies.

The fight for survival is paramount when it comes to food, and most horses will protect their own interests. The underdogs become the bullied, and may fall by the wayside. In domesticity man can control the food he gives, and can look after those that are threatened by others. He needs to do this, as they will not look after themselves.

> The desire for food is so great that a mare will chase off her own foal if she feels the need for it herself.

Bullying comes in various forms. It may start with a threatening expression with the ears back and the lips curled; the next step is to bite, and finally to kick. These actions can also be applied to humans, and depending on their reaction will be developed or quashed.

If the horse finds he receives punishment for his bullying tactics he will soon abandon them: but should he discover that correction is faint-hearted, he may continue and even get worse. A similar situation can occur with those animals

Protectiveness

A tremendous change of personality can take place if one animal wishes to protect another. This happens chiefly with mares who have, or have had, foals. Not only does a mare want to protect her young from prey but also from other mares who may wish to take it over, or from humans who try to interfere with her natural instincts. In these cases the most sweet-tempered animal can appear quite savage, biting or kicking other animals or people who get too close. A knowledgeable person will be able to cope with this by catching the mare and holding her while the foal is given attention. During this time consideration should be given to the mare who will be feeling vulnerable and may be aggressive.

Many mares who have had foals develop a protective attitude towards some other horse, obviously feeling the necessity to mother something. This can be tiresome if they become too attached and a weaning process may be necessary. Protectiveness can be a useful trait as long as it does not get out of control, and sometimes a firm hand has to be taken, bearing in mind that the maternal instinct is very strong and cannot, and should not, be entirely crushed.

Intimidation

Horses sometimes have curious ways of intimidating their owners and it could be said that most will try some form of intimidation during their lives; whether or not it develops into something really unpleasant depends on the owner's response. Thus if he allows himself to be intimidated the horse will quickly realize this and follow up his advantage. But if it is dealt with firmly and with ingenuity at the outset, the horse will soon realize that his action is a mistake and he will give it up.

Once a horse has learned to intimidate, his attitude will be difficult to eradicate and will have to be controlled with care and skill. One horse I owned had the habit of attacking you if you walked out of his stable with your back to him; but if you walked out facing him he did not try it on. It was no use being aggressive because this only made him worse, but the method we adopted never caused any trouble. In every other way this horse was kind, but he had obviously got away with this odd behaviour at some time in his past. If I had not worked out this safe compromise I might have been injured and the horse branded as a brute – and he might never have become an international dressage horse!

who think they can get what they want by using their strength. If they are allowed to barge about trampling everything in their path they will continue to do so.

A horse is not naturally nasty and will only become one if he discovers that by using certain tactics he can have his own way. One cause of bullying humans results from too many titbits, which can cause the horse to expect them; when he does not get them he will be angry.

Throwing Food About

There may be several causes for this annoying habit. One could be that the teeth need attention: it is the owner's responsibility to keep a check on the state of his horse's mouth. He should check for sores or sharp teeth, and at least be aware that an injury of the mouth could put the horse off his food.

Sometimes the cause is simply that the bucket or manger is dirty and needs a good scrub. Stale food stuck to the sides gives off an unpleasantly rank smell that certainly could put the horse off. All bins, buckets and mangers should be cleaned daily.

Another reason could be that the horse does not like what he is eating. No one horse is the same as another, and although the same basic diet may be fed to a stable of twenty horses, there will always be one or two that have to be fed something different. It is just a case of finding out what.

Considering that horses like their food so much it may seem odd that they should apparently be so blasé as to waste it, but there are always some who break the rules as well as those who have a legitimate reason.

Fear of the Vet or Farrier

This phobia has already been discussed, but it is so common that the subject deserves further mention. Smell is the biggest barrier and the one that has to be overcome first. Wise owners will introduce these persons to their animals as early in their lives as possible, and preferably before they need attention. In this way the young animal will become accustomed to

A strange quirk that developed in a young horse belonging to a friend was that every time the farrier appeared the horse had a nosebleed! This phenomenon took place several times and was presumably connected to an anxiety that stressed blood vessels in the nasal passages. It was not severe and as the horse became more confident the condition disappeared.

them so that eventually, when their feet have to be trimmed or shod or they have to have their first injections, their fear is minimized.

Mane and Tail Pulling; Bathing

As owners we like to see our horses as smartly turned out as possible, and so we trim them up regularly and pull their manes and tails. Some do not mind this at all and put up with our ministrations without objection; others, however, hate it, finding it far too painful to put up with. In these cases it may be wiser and kinder to use a thinning knife, or merely to cut off the hair; it can be done in such a way that it does not look 'chopped'.

Some horses also object to being bathed prior to a show, although on the whole I have never found a horse that really would not accept the procedure once it understood what was happening. As with all handling, a sensible, gradual approach should be adopted.

Tumours

Fortunately very rare in occurrence,

Fighting with the horse on the ground for whatever reason does not make for a good relationship, and each owner should consider his horse's sensitivity and decide for himself whether he is being fair to it.

Twitching

Although I do not like twitching and would not advocate its use, most of us have at some time or another used it as a last resort as a way to quieten a horse in order to clip it, cover it by the stallion, shoe it, or pull its mane or tail. The method of winding a cord round the horse's upper lip and tightening it has been used for years, and is an effective way of exercising extra control when simply holding the horse does not work. Scientific research has established that the action of the twitch releases chemicals that have a tranquillizing effect on the horse; this is known as the 'endorphin reaction'. Certainly when a twitch is applied most animals stand quite calmly, although I have known several on whom it certainly did not have a fully tranquillizing effect. I personally would never twitch the ears, and consider it to be a dangerous and cruel practice.

strange or problem behaviour sometimes turns out to be caused by a tumour of the brain. I have known three cases and all were irreconcilable, the horses ultimately having to be put down. In their lifetime they undoubtedly experienced a degree of suffering because we could not explain their irrational behaviour. One was a head shaker whose habit sometimes became so violent when ridden that it would try to rub the bridle off altogether. For some time the owner was of the opinion that the horse was merely irritated by the leather, by flies or by pollen. Some head shakers are affected by sunlight, and have few problems during the winter months. This one, however, rapidly deteriorated and was finally diagnosed as having a tumour. A subsequent post mortem revealed this to be correct.

Another case was a Thoroughbred horse that had come out of racing. It was sent to my friend for re-breaking as it had become rather naughty, and as it was a young horse he decided to start at the beginning and put it on the lunge. On the very first day it came out, went forwards for a couple of circles and then stopped dead, reared up and fell over backwards. This happened many times until finally my friend decided to abandon the exercise. This horse also had a tumour.

Clearly in these cases no amount of understanding would have helped, but it is important to realize that such things do occur. If there is ever doubt as to how to proceed in unusual circumstances, veterinary advice should be sought, even if only to eliminate this possibility.

Man's Response

Learn to anticipate those occasions when the horse could feel too restricted, or might be worried by the circumstances he finds himself in; this is the best way to help those suffering anxiety.

Knowing when to call the vet is important, as is also feeding suitable substances to those horses more liable to nervous problems.

General handling is basically common sense combined with knowledge of the horse's needs.

CHAPTER 12

The Horse under Saddle

Fitting Tack

Being dressed up in all manner of equipment is an aspect of the domesticated horse's life that the horse himself often finds hard to accept. Essentially a 'free spirit', not only is it hard for him to submit to the physical restriction of saddle and bridle, it is also difficult for his mind to take in, especially if pain is involved.

Before he is asked to carry a saddle he will first have to become used to a cavesson and a roller, as used for lungeing. Introduced sensibly the roller should not cause a problem, although a horse will object if it is tightened too suddenly or if it is left too loose so that it slips about; there is nothing more frightening for a young horse than to find himself with a loose roller flapping round his belly or back legs. No doubt he imagines he is being attacked by some evil creature, but even by flying off bucking or by kicking, his two instinctive means of defending himself, he cannot rid himself of it. Many problems in saddling or backing can be traced back to badly put on rollers. It is a good idea to attach a breast-girth or breastplate to the roller to prevent it slipping back.

Side-reins may be introduced next, attached from the cavesson to the roller in order to give the horse an idea of going forwards to a contact, which he will have to accept later on when being ridden.

Great care must be taken in fitting the side-reins, however, because it is at this point that the horse will find out what it is like to be relatively restricted; and if he panics at this stage he may fall backwards or rear and slip over, and much harm will be done. It is therefore most important that the side-reins are not too tight, particularly to start with; in fact at first the side-reins can be quite loose, the lightest contact possible. I saw a spectacular 'flip over' once when a pony wearing side-reins for the first time, suddenly feeling the contact on his mouth, leaped right off the ground, somersaulting onto its back. Clearly this is undesirable and dangerous, and was very likely caused by the side-reins being adjusted much too tightly. Being in a position to send the horse forwards immediately is also essential when side-reins are attached, as once he has become accustomed to the rein-contact he will settle down happily.

Bitting

Many problems arise from bitting, most of which derive from thoughtless or unsympathetic riding. However, it is very important to fit any bit correctly, and to be certain that the horse is comfortable. The pain that a bit can inflict undoubtedly contributes to any resentment a horse may show against his rider, which he will display by throwing his head about,

This bridle fits well and the horse looks happy and comfortable.

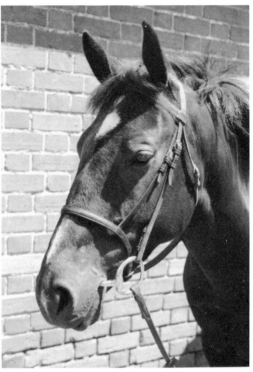

Many people ride in bits that are too large for their horse's mouth. This is horribly uncomfortable for the horse and causes training problems.

opening his mouth, putting his tongue out and so on. On the whole, using a stronger bit or any other method of trying to make the horse 'give' to the rider is a false security, and many are downright cruel.

Gadgets and their Effect

Many of the gadgets that owners use to

So many horses suffer because their riders are not patient enough to train them properly, taking short cuts rather than spending the time required to achieve an objective.

force their horse into an outline are cruel to the horse both mentally and physically. Just how much mental suffering a horse is sometimes obliged to endure was forcibly brought home to me when I watched a famous show jumper lungeing his horse in a sharp bit over a fence at a show recently. The wretched animal was trussed up so tightly in order to make him 'round his back' that he could barely jump the fence. His mouth was cut and his eyes glazed, and his spirit seemed altogether humbled and destroyed. To my mind, no prize whatsoever justifies that sort of oppressive treatment of a horse.

Resentment to the bit or the rider's hands is shown by the horse by throwing his head up and opening his mouth.

This horse is clearly expressing anxiety. His head is up, his ears are back and his tail is swishing.

A sad picture this, as although the horse has submitted he is plainly unhappy.
His eyes, ears and tail are all giving signs of displeasure.

Having 'given in' to the inevitable the horse is now resigned, but he has now
found an alternative way to avoid the bit by overbending.

The horse is a little happier in this picture and is perhaps beginning to understand his rider but the position of his ears tell us that he is still not sure.

I saw the same dispirited expression on the face of a horse in Germany: it was being ridden through the same exercise again and again in a strong curb bit; the rider had sharp spurs and was relentless in his demands. At first the horse fought him, but after a very considerable time it not only gave in but showed the same glazed expression, drooping ears and total lack of enthusiasm or interest that I had seen before.

Fortunately this kind of riding is not particularly prevalent, although I have encountered it to a certain extent when judging dressage. What you do sometimes see are well trained horses ridden by less experienced riders, and the confusion they feel is all too evident in their eyes and expression as they try to do the job they know but are prevented from doing so by ignorant riding.

To kill a horse's natural spirit, for whatever reason, is in my opinion unforgivable.

The Double Bridle

When first introduced this can be quite a traumatic experience for the horse unless the bits fit well and the rider knows how to use them. It is not hard to imagine the discomfort and the feeling of restriction that can be caused if the curb is over-used. Furthermore, many people simply do not realize the damage that a badly fitting jointed bit or a high port can do to the roof of the horse's mouth. It is significant that when in pain, the horse will generally put his head up to relieve himself; this is just the opposite of what the rider intends by putting on the double in the first place.

When introducing the horse to a double bridle it should be done without pressure

Many horses resent double bridle bits to start with because they are quite a mouthful. Do not forget they are more severe than a snaffle and need tactful use.

from the curb until the horse is happy with the feel of the two bits. The rider must learn to hold the reins correctly, and be able to adjust the tension. Many animals, on meeting the restriction imposed by their rider via a strong hold, will actually try to go faster and may lean on the bit more. In this way they avoid some of the action of the bit and can therefore evade the rider's wishes.

All equipment should be introduced to the horse with care and consideration for his feelings; it should then be used with tact and common sense.

Backing

This stage of the horse's training is crucial, and any problems now will have far-reaching effects. The horse will by this time have been taught to submit to the wearing of a bridle and saddle, and he should have been taught to obey voice commands made on the lunge or long reins. If he has not been upset or frightened thus far, the leaning over process or the rider actually sitting on him, should not worry him. However, it is important that the rider is legged up at this stage, because if the saddle slips or the rider's weight is put more on one side, it may bother the horse.

With the help of a person on the ground whose voice the horse knows, he may then be gradually ridden away, first on the lunge so that the association of familiar word commands still applies and later on his own. However, until the voice commands are sufficiently associated with the hand and leg aids in the horse's mind, he should not be ridden outside an enclosed area.

When he has fully grasped the meaning of the simple 'aids' – go, turn and stop – he may be ridden out on the roads (if suitable), preferably in company with an older horse.

His mental education can now develop together with his physical fitness.

Schooling Area and Exercises

Ideally the horse should have his first lessons in a quiet area with no distractions, preferably fenced so that he is contained. His mind and body will best be able to develop from work 'on the flat' in an arena of no less than 40m x 20m with a good surface. The material of the latter is a personal preference, but whatever is chosen it should provide the horse with a safe footing with no risk of slipping, and it should not be too deep. Even willing horses will become downhearted at having to struggle through deep sand, and equally they will very quickly go off the idea of work if they tread on anything hard.

This picture shows a quiet and suitable environment for schooling with plenty of room.

Be careful when training not to cause trouble by leaving hazardous poles or other objects lying around.

School exercises are designed to encourage balance and suppleness, and if ridden correctly provide the horse with the best chance to take in what he is being asked. Such exercises as straight lines, circles, loops and serpentines, and also extensions, collection and all lateral work, are taught to enhance suppleness but they must be combined with energy and good acceptance of the aids. In this way the horse's mind is properly prepared for his future, and his body is able to respond.

Discipline

Right from the start of training the horse should be aware of his position, that he will not be allowed to behave just as he pleases, but must obey certain rules. Thus displays of exuberance while being ridden will not be allowed as they could be dangerous to the rider.

In order that the horse's spirit does not become too oppressed by over-discipline, a degree of compromise may at first be allowed, provided it does not cause any possible hazard. In general, however, the horse must learn to do as he is told, and as long as he is clear what this is, he will usually comply. When he responds in the right way he should be rewarded by a pat on the neck and a praising voice; like this he will soon learn that when his rider is pleased with his efforts his life is pleasant, and he will behave accordingly.

Some horses react badly to discipline, and will not submit easily. This is natural enough, but this sort may take longer to train or need a firmer line taken.

Punishment

A horse is reprimanded either by use of the voice, or by a firmer use of the aids. Using the voice as a punishment can be very effective if the horse knows the implications of the different voice tones, and many will respond to the voice alone.

If a horse requires firmer aids, the rider will use his legs backed up with a whip and spurs if and when necessary. These should never be used in isolation, but only in addition to aids already being given.

The most important thing about giving punishment is to make it clear to the horse *why* it is being given – it is essential that the horse understands the reason for the reprimand and this will only come about by association. In other words he must be punished for his wrongdoings *at the time* and not later.

> Thrashing a horse – which some people do – is unnecessary and can be very cruel. Nor should a horse *ever* be hit round the head; I have known several blinded in this way.

Following any sort of punishment the horse should then be praised for any small improvement. He will soon grasp the point, making the correction worthwhile.

Of course there are times when a horse is more receptive to corrections than others, and it is important that each rider learns when it is propitious to confront his horse. If he is being difficult, he is not being so just for the sake of it, and there are several reasons why he might be objecting:

> A horse can tolerate a relatively high degree of pain, although some are more sensitive than others; these should certainly not need strong correction. Other, less sensitive horses can become quite 'mulish' as a result of over-correction, and some learn to switch off altogether; with these, whatever the rider does, it will be ineffective. We bought a beautiful horse once that had been cruelly handled and had suffered many beatings in the past. We were fully prepared to give him all the time he needed to regain his trust in the human race, made a special effort in the stable to build a rapport, and started his training from the beginning. All was to no avail. This was a tremendous disappointment to us, and to him a disaster, as he was clearly useless as a riding horse.

- He has never done the exercise before.
- He does not understand the exercise.
- The way he is being asked is not clear.
- He has done the exercise before but the aids given were not the ones used on the previous occasion.
- He is not fit enough for the exercise.
- It is beyond his capability.
- He is distracted by other activities.
- He is over-excited and tense.
- He is in pain.

All these reasons can affect a horse's response, and it is the rider's responsibility to use this 'check-list' to ensure that he has given the horse every possible chance before any punishment is inflicted.

Obstinacy

Stubbornness evolves for certain reasons. Some horses are inherently lazy and simply do not wish to make the effort required of them; or it may be that they have the sort of brain that works slowly, needing time to absorb information and translate it into action. Both of these causes can be aggravating to a trainer but are relatively easily assessed.

There is another cause for stubbornness, and that is the animal who, the more it is pressured, the more it switches its mind off to the nagging it is receiving, the outcome of which is an obstinate refusal to cooperate. Fortunately this is rare, as there is nothing more hopeless than trying to teach a horse which is mentally switched off! When this happens the brain refuses to receive or send signals and the animal becomes almost inanimate. In this circumstance neither spur nor whip have any effect and the usefulness of the animal may be over. The ones I have known who have reached this sad state have done so because they have physically or mentally been unable to do what they were asked, and have therefore retreated into a state of blankness. This always applies if an animal has been continually forced to do something against its will, either because it is difficult or there is a lack of understanding or an active dislike. Some will continue with reluctance, but there are a few who will decide that enough is enough.

Force is never acceptable to horses or humans although it is sometimes necessary, but it should never become the only answer to achieve results if patience and ingenuity will work instead.

Communication in Training

Whatever lesson the horse is being taught, the rider must make it plain exactly what

he wants. His method of 'speaking' to the horse is mainly through his body, leg and hand aids, with some help from the voice. Obviously if his position is incorrect the aids cannot be applied correctly or effectively, and in this case the messages sent to the horse's brain will be jumbled or inadequate and he will therefore find it hard to give a proper answer. A high percentage of a horse's incorrect responses are due to poor communication; the other percentage may be because the horse is dull or perhaps upset.

Horses vary a good deal in their individual ability to respond. Some will be quick, others slow, but whichever it is it must be understood by each owner and allowance made. Thus it is no good expecting a clearly less intelligent horse to learn his lesson as quickly as the one that thinks faster. The slow one will need more repetition to enable him to grasp a point. Nevertheless, once the slow learners have finally understood something they retain this knowledge very well; just because they are slow does not mean that their memory is less able than the clever horse.

In fact the slower learners have an

Horses learn from a system of repetition and reward, and one is no good without the other. Many riders do not appreciate sufficiently the importance of rewarding the horse, which may be vocal praise or with a pat. Nor do they reward often enough; during early training praising the horse can hardly be overdone, although as he learns what is wanted it becomes less necessary. Finally as the rapport between horse and rider becomes more firmly established, the horse's reward for obeying his rider comes from a 'lightening' of the aids.

advantage in some ways, in that because they often tend to be lazier they don't bother to think of anything else, whereas the 'bright' horse is always on the lookout for something new. Often the more intelligent the animal the cleverer the rider has to be, as not only must he teach the horse what he wants, but he must also be one jump ahead!

Although much repetition is important in order for the horse to be clear in his mind, there is also a danger that if overdone he will become bored and apathetic in his work. Riders who go endlessly round in twenty-metre circles are doing their horses no favours. In fact to the horse it is rather like being on a treadmill which in time becomes a mindless occupation. Similarly, those riders who jump their horses incessantly over the same fence or fences are inviting trouble, as their animals become sick of doing the same thing over and over again.

Variety is important as long as the animal is prepared properly. Changing quickly from one movement or exercise to another can be equally muddling to the horse, especially if he is made to do this in an unbalanced way.

Because the messages given by the rider necessarily take a while to reach the horse's brain, time should always be allowed for a response to be made. Moreover all mental responses have to be

Horses are easily unbalanced by their riders. This is a classic example. The rider is sitting 'on the withers', thereby placing all her weight on the horse's forehand.

THE HORSE UNDER SADDLE

This rider also is causing her horse difficulties as she is throwing her body up his neck, so putting her weight onto his shoulders.

effected by the limbs concerned, which in the horse's case involves a lot of organization.

Because of the horse's build he is easily unbalanced, especially when additionally hindered by his rider. It is therefore important for him that his rider sits on him in such a way as to assist him to balance, thereby making it easier for him to respond in the best way possible. Also, the horse will need to be placed in a position from which he can best comply to whatever he is being asked to do. Thus he must be given the chance to see where he is going, and so should be placed either straight or following a curved line depending on the movement or situation.

He should be asked to travel at a speed which he can control himself and be controlled. He should be given plenty of warning of what is to come, and be given the time to prepare himself.

All these arrangements are best made for the horse by training him on the flat, using a system of exercises designed to develop his physique and his memory bank. From sound groundwork the horse will have the best opportunity to proceed to any area of work that his rider wishes.

Pressure

In their own anxiety to 'get on', some riders over-pressurize their horses.

On the other hand this rider is giving the horse the best possible chance by sitting in a balanced position allowing freedom of the horse's head and neck.

It is important to appreciate that the horse can suffer mental trauma as a result of too much pressure. A young horse I was watching recently worked well for twenty minutes, but his rider was apparently not satisfied and kept going round and round her school until the animal was in a muck sweat. Finally it started to whinny frantically in the same way as a foal calls desperately to its mother. I did not doubt that this was a 'cry for help', an urgent plea to be relieved from an intolerable situation. Sadly the rider seemed quite oblivious to her horse's state of mind; by then it was in such a mental state that no good was coming from the work at all.

I have encountered this with other horses, and on each occasion there has been no question of being able to 'ride through' the difficulty; the animal had to be allowed to relax, and to come out again another day.

Fitness

Much of the horse's mental willingness will depend on his physical ability to be able to do what he is asked, something which riders do not always take into account. Feeding is of prime importance, and getting this right for each individual horse takes trial and error. Placid horses for instance may well need a diet that will pep them up, whereas an excitable type may do better with more bulk feed and fewer 'shorts' (concentrates).

Much disappointment on the part of the rider could be avoided if more importance was placed on getting the horse fit. A fat horse will be just as handicapped as a thin one in its ability to respond to its rider as required: the stress and strain involved is enormous when it is either puffing round in an overweight condition or dragging round with its ribs hanging out. The suffering that some people cause their animals is very sad to see, and no excuse is acceptable.

It is also important to realize that a horse considered fit enough to work at home may not be fit enough for the additional work and stress involved at a competition. Excitement and anxiety can take a considerable physical and mental toll, and although the horse will have to learn to come through the mental angle, physically he must be fit enough to do so

There are, of course, specialist areas of riding (or driving), where extra fitness is needed, such as racing, polo or eventing. Experts in these fields will be aware of the necessity for a fit horse, but those with less knowledge should give some thought for the horse's mental anguish as he tries his best when physically he is not able to accomplish what is asked of him. His willingness and inherent stamina can often lead to him breaking down as tendons and joints try to take the strain. To my mind it is not fair to trade on the fact that the horse is a strong animal: his strength can only be effective if his physical fitness has been steadily built up, and his mental health also depends on this physical fitness.

Development

Teaching the horse what we want him to do involves a great deal of hard work and

In certain areas of riding extra fitness is needed. This driving horse looks in good condition to do the job he has to do.

dedication, especially if we have high goals. Building up his ability depends on a systematic approach to training whereby he is given progressively more difficult lessons.

As his understanding of the work increases, a certain rapport between him and his rider gradually evolves and strengthens. This often goes in stages, rising quite suddenly as enlightenment occurs, but 'plateau-ing out' from time to time. Riders often become discouraged if they remain on the 'plateau' for too long, and there is a risk that both parties will become bored. This is when perhaps both need a change of scene of some kind, a complete break from schooling, a short holiday, or some different activity altogether.

Each person will have a general riding routine which he or she will want to keep to as it is part of a training programme; but the horse's brain can only absorb so much at one time and may reach a point where it is rather like a saturated sponge, having taken in all it can. Given a rest – a day, or a few days – and it will be ready to start again. As an owner it is important therefore to realize that the horse really will need his mental break just as much as you do, and to allow for it.

Problems

An enormous variety of problems arise from training, many of which are essentially physical but which by association become a mental problem also.

Bridle Lameness

This is when a horse appears to be lame or is irregular in his stride; however, it is due to stiffness rather than real lameness. The answer is to make the horse more supple, but I have known one horse which on discovering that if he 'put it on' was allowed back to his stable, thus using the problem to his advantage.

Clearly it is important to make sure that the horse is sound in the first place, and if he is, then to work him through the problem.

Brushing

The hoof on one side of the horse may knock the hoof, fetlock or leg on the opposite side. Horses which are very narrow or which are unfit may do this, and it is annoying because it may cause them to become lame.

Although a horse would not be able to do this deliberately, it can happen if he is too bored or idle to go properly.

Bolting

Horses that take off when being ridden may do so because they are anxious to catch up with a pal, having got left behind; or because they are frightened and are running away.

If the horse is running away, the situation is highly dangerous for everyone concerned as he will not be thinking properly at all, his only intention being to get away from whatever frightened him. Even his inborn self-preservation is at risk. Fortunately that sort of bolting is rare, and the more usual form is a short burst of uncontrolled energy. Even that can cause a difficult situation, however, and can be avoided only by thorough training – whereby the aids really are effective – and by anticipation of possible causes.

Cold Back

Many horses will sink their back when a saddle is first put on or when a rider first mounts. Initially no doubt this occurs as a result of discomfort or pain, but knowing this, the horse may then try to avoid the situation altogether by fidgeting or walking off. This can develop into a problem with mounting, which may become impossible if the pain that the horse is anticipating develops in his mind.

Bucking

Some horses discover that a good buck will dislodge their rider, and use this to their own advantage. In the wild, the best way to remove a predator pouncing on their back was to buck until it was dislodged, so really this reaction is entirely natural! If his saddle slips or his rider bounces about, or if anything else unusual happens, it could make the horse want to rid himself of this burden on his back.

A horse will buck when he is turned out in order to express excitement; it is also a purely natural way to give himself extra physical relief. When ridden, however, the horse must learn that he has nothing to fear from his rider, and that he may not express himself in this way.

Forging

The toe of a hind shoe clicks against the heel of the opposite fore shoe. Although this can be irritating for the rider or anyone watching the horse, it has no particularly dangerous implications. However, it can be due to a lack of interest on the part of the horse or because he is unbalanced; as already mentioned, any

Rain

In their natural state, horses cope with bad weather by taking shelter from woodland or hedgerow. With these natural windbreaks or if they are out in the open, they will stand tail-on to the rain or wind, the thick tail hair giving some protection; and if they stand with lowered heads, much of the weather passes over them. Thick hair and oil in the coat stops the rain from penetrating through to the skin.

Horses which are kept stabled are invariably robbed of this natural protection: because they wear rugs the whole time, hair growth is suppressed, and the horse is usually clipped. Also tails are often pulled. When it rains or the wind blows, any horse will try to turn his back to it, and this practice can present problems in training. Sometimes it is feasible to go along with this, but at other times it may be inconvenient or even impossible. Whilst understanding the horse's dilemma, owners may have to insist on discipline over this matter; and most horses will accept rain driving into their faces if taught that they must do so.

There are a few horses who dislike rain on their backs and become very difficult. We had one such horse which had been imported from a part of the world where there is very little rain and where the horses are barned. We did not know this when we first bought him, and could not understand his paranoia when a few drops of rain fell on his back. He became quite unruly when this occurred and we began to wonder if he had a mental problem. In a sense he had as, when we enquired, we discovered that he had never been out in the rain in his life! He obviously found it a frightening experience but eventually learnt to cope with the problem. Living in Britain he had to do so!

lack of balance can adversely affect the horse because his limbs are relatively slow-moving anyway. Furthermore it may be an indication that he is probably bored, may be unfit and is quite probably not properly prepared.

Rearing and Napping

Napping comes in many guises, from a relatively passive resistance to outright stubbornness or violent objection. Generally the horse has discovered, probably by accident, that something he does makes his rider 'back off' or even give up asking a question that he doesn't really want to answer. The reason may be physical or it may have happened as the result of a confusion over the 'aids', but whatever it is, once the horse has discovered a way to take the upper hand, the rider is in a vulnerable position. Regaining the advantage can be difficult – sometimes impossible – and often not worth the effort if the 'nap' is confirmed.

The rider should prevent this behaviour in the first place by not giving the horse the opportunity to learn about it, and by being aware of the sort of situation that might cause it.

Refusing Fences

Some horses can indeed learn to be nappy and so avoid what is to them an unpleasant experience; but this is not necessarily the only reason for their nappiness. There are plenty of genuine reasons why the horse might refuse a fence such as being overfaced, or presented with some new obstacle he has not seen before. Also, if the rider is half-hearted he may see no reason to jump!

Going from light into dark has already

Although this horse has no rider on it, it is easy to see how vulnerable he would be. Once the horse is in this position he has the upper hand.

been mentioned in Chapter 2, and can be quite a problem when jumping out of a sunlit field into a dark wood. Jumping into water is often a problem for the horse, too, as he is not sure of the safety of the landing; most horses will instinctively test the ground before they venture into it, given the chance. And some will not go into water at all, even though nowadays training a horse to go into water is all part of the system.

It is understandable, I think, to accept that not only do we have to bring our horses along gradually and introduce new things to them using common sense, but also to remember that they do have strong urges of their own that guide their minds.

When presented with reluctance or napping the rider should assess the cause but then be prepared to take a firm line.

Shying

Generally horses shy for good reason, or so they consider. Something will have frightened them and to move or run away from it, is a natural response. It becomes a problem when the horse finds that, as a result of his actions, he can avoid doing what his rider wants. It becomes a mild form of 'napping', and some undoubtedly do this.

I have had horses which appear to see things that are not there, and who shy for no reason. Upon investigation some were discovered to have faulty sight, a condition which was confirmed by the vet. Quite often the shadows or patterns the horse sees mean something to him, even if they don't to us, and our impatience over this apparent nonsense worries him, making him worse. This can easily develop into a neurosis as the horse anticipates our unsympathetic reactions to his fears.

Tensions and Resistances

Whenever a horse feels tension or anxiety for whatever reason, there is likely to be opposition towards the rider. Anxiety can be caused by imaginary fears or real ones, fears that have become an issue in his mind.

If he anticipates pain, or an impatient reaction from his rider, he is likely to be tense. His resistance may be fairly mild,

---

Sneezing
While being ridden the horse may learn that this entirely natural action can result in him gaining control. And if he sneezes frequently his rider may rest him, or he may simply be able to rid himself of the rein contact.

Although he should be allowed to sneeze if essential, it must certainly not be excessive.

Horses soon discover whether their riders are determined or not and some will find a way of avoiding what they are being asked.

expressing itself in teeth grinding or tail swishing; or it can be far more obvious, with ears laid back, eyes showing their whites, even kicking against the aids. Also there will be bit evasions such as the mouth hanging open or the tongue coming over the bit, or hanging out of the side of the mouth. The horse may tilt his head to avoid pressure, he may twist his neck and overbend, and even throw himself about.

However, all this is done because he is uncomfortable and is trying to find some way out of that discomfort. As a last resort he may try to rid himself of a rider he dislikes, perhaps like a pony I once had, which learned that if she cantered off and then stopped dead ducking her right shoulder, her rider instantly fell off! Once learned this sort of trick is ingrained in the horse's mind and will undoubtedly be used again.

Some problems certainly do occur because young horses are teething, or older ones have a sharp tooth catching on

Wolf teeth do sometimes cause discomfort and have to be removed by a professional. However, there are many problems that are blamed on the horse having wolf teeth which are nothing to do with them at all: it is poor riding that is at fault.

the side of the mouth. If the horse is being especially awkward when ridden, it is always wise to check his mouth.

Man's Response

Training horses is a hard job; re-training them is harder. Whatever we do with our animals, we should give them the benefit of the doubt first. Only if we are sure that our actions have been properly thought out and executed, may we expect to get the response we asked for.

CHAPTER 13

Sympathy and Sensitivity

The late Colonel Jack Hance always maintained that the period of time needed for a rider and horse to get to know each other was a minimum of two years. During my time with horses, the more I have seen, the more I agree with this remark. Dealers and some professionals who produce horses will argue that they have not got the time to do this, as the horses have to be sold or brought out ready for the show ring more quickly. I understand their dilemma, but there are many others not in this position who are able to spend the time but do not do so.

A rushed job cannot be as satisfactory as one over which more care has been taken, because if short cuts are used there is not such a good chance to build up any rapport. Only those owners who are patient and who are prepared to devote considerable time to their horse can expect to 'bond' with him to any high degree. From a true 'bonding', an almost telepathic closeness can evolve, where such an understanding exists between horses and rider that the horse will respond to the slightest of signals.

Friendship Begins on the Ground

Each owner having deliberated on his own particular horse's needs will, if he has observed diligently, earn its trust, and this is the first step towards a close relationship.

The horse must know that he will never be put into a frightening situation, nor be irrevocably hurt in any way. He will be helped through his panicky moments and new experiences from the confidence you can give him, and if he has to be punished

Friendship begins on the ground.

he must know that this is followed by appreciation. Remember that erratic behaviour on our part or inconsistency is very puzzling for the horse, and he cannot be expected to understand.

> Sensitivity works both ways. We should be able to use ours to work out the horse's feelings, as he will certainly be aware of ours. Emotion plays a big part in our sensitivity and how we react towards the horse.

Anger

When we are irritated or angry we are not entirely in control of ourselves, and the result is often impatience, either with ourselves or with the horse. In our frustration we generally react badly using rough, ill thought out aids. Plainly this sort of reaction is no good to the horse because he suddenly receives signals that are different or harsh and he doesn't know why, and his confusion will cause him to respond in a muddled way which will only add to an already distressing situation. He cannot work out what is wanted, and only clear directions can clarify the matter for him.

Tears and Frustration

All those who work with horses have probably felt like weeping at some time even if they haven't actually done so. Training animals is not easy and many of us will often feel frustration and disappointment because of our inadequacy. In fact horses are well aware when we are upset, espe-

cially if they know us well. Just as we comfort the horse when he is upset, so we can derive much from him, simply because he *is* our friend.

Helping each other through a crisis is all part of the bonding process, and it is amazing how much help our horses can give us in practical ways, such as getting us over a difficult fence, as well as soothing our shattered emotions just by their presence.

Fears

Certainly horses know when we are fearful. We give the game away by being tentative or negative or simply by perspiring. A nasty-tempered horse will soon sense fear if the person attempting to handle it does not approach confidently and handle it firmly. People who shout at horses or hit them are usually frightened of them, and although this might momentarily cause the horse to 'back off', he will still sense the nervousness behind it.

Nervous riders who clutch at their horse's mouths, perch forwards and fail to give firm directions are compromising their authority, and the horse will soon take advantage of the fact that he is not going to be made to work. His will soon becomes dominant over his rider, and the habit of napping often starts in this way.

> **Love**
> By giving love and affection to our horses we are inviting their trust and confidence in us. It may not be an emotion that they actually experience but their respect for us will provide the kind of relationship where mutual appreciation exists.

Confidence

We can only give confidence if we ourselves are confident that what we are doing or asking the horse to do is correct, and a horse will soon be able to tell if his rider is confident from the signals he receives. Sometimes he must be made to do things he doesn't want to do, but having found he is quite capable, he will then be perfectly willing.

If he receives rather negative, vague commands his response may be negative. Learning how to give confident commands that combine a positive attitude with a sympathetic one requires a good deal of experience, but the horse needs this combination if he is to perform satisfactorily for us.

Determination

Our attitude towards a particular goal, whether it be leading our horse in from the field or riding him round a three-day-event, will determine his responses. In the course of his training, a horse will quickly learn to recognize and distinguish between a true resolve on the part of his rider or a weak one.

Sometimes he will be stubborn, determined to resist his rider – and some horses can be exceedingly stubborn. They are generally the type which are idle by nature and rather slow to learn, and if that idleness combines with a tendency to nap, then real trouble lies ahead. The answer is to be as firm as possible in the first place so there is no chance for negative thoughts to evolve.

Anticipation

Many problems could be avoided if we could only anticipate them more readily. For example, a horse is quite often baffled because he believes that something specific is about to take place which he prepares for, only to find that he is either not going to do it, or he does it and is then punished.

This often happens in training when the horse has been taught a particular exercise in a particular place. This method of teaching him is good, as he can more readily grasp what is being asked if it is repeated in the same place, but it clearly creates a problem if the horse is not truly listening to his rider, or if the signals he receives are distorted.

When a horse anticipates he may succeed in doing what he expected to do, but he may also at the last moment, be unsure. Thus his reaction will be somewhat muddled, and this will in turn confuse the rider – and so there evolves a moment of discord where neither is in control. In this situation the rider must take the responsibility for a recovery by remaining calm in order that the horse may be made receptive to correction.

There are also situations when the horse anticipates pain. We often cause our horses to become headshy or nervous by our own inadvertent action, such as raising a hand too sharply; and of course once a punishment has been given in a specific circumstance the horse will remember it and will anticipate it again. Therefore every action we make should be thought out beforehand, because even if we do not remember what we have done, the horse will.

Concentration

It is plain that if we do not give full attention to what we are doing then we cannot expect the horse to concentrate either. Persuading him to listen requires communication either from the voice or from the aids, and quite often just talking to the horse, especially if he is familiar with the voice concerned, will bring his mind to bear on what is at hand. Successfully gaining his attention by way of the aids requires the coordinated use of legs and hands, and contact from both. The rider's legs should always be in contact with the horse's sides, and there should be a steady elastic tension from the hands via the reins to the horse's mouth; only in this way can messages be sent satisfactorily. The rider is then responsible for being consistent in the messages he sends.

Loss of concentration can also derive from boredom, and generally arises if the rider is lacking in imagination or knowledge and doesn't give his horse enough variation.

Horses which persistently call out to each other can be very trying, and the habit a real problem at a competition. Young horses or entires are most prone to the distraction of others, but a number of horses will call constantly to their friends. They may do this because they feel insecure in a strange situation, or they may want to be reassured that their friend is nearby. To whinny is a primitive instinct for the purpose of communication, and only by giving the horse confidence and by making him obedient can we overcome this problem.

It is understandable that the horse should want to look about, especially in a strange place. He will want to establish for himself the possible dangers, and determine whether what he hears or sees is of interest to him. As he hears sounds long before we do, being able to anticipate when he is likely to lose concentration for this reason is almost impossible; but whilst we may not be able to prevent it, we should, from our own rapport with him, regain it quickly.

New sights or experiences will cause our horses to look about, and to a degree this must be allowed. Once he has accepted the situation, however, he should be expected to give attention to his rider – but he will only do so if he is made to.

Discipline

A horse will readily accept discipline if he knows *why* he is being disciplined. In fact horses actually seem to *like* to be disciplined, apparently finding a certain security from it. They know where they stand, and in any society this is a necessity.

Unruly behaviour cannot be tolerated

Misinterpretation

Even the horse with his remarkable memory is not infallible, and does make mistakes sometimes. When he does, he often knows he has, and becomes quite upset as a result. He may then lose control of himself, and in addition may become anxious because he expects a reprimand.

If he has made a genuine mistake he should never be punished but allowed a second chance. If he persistently misinterprets then he should be returned to an easier lesson and made to pay attention to what he is being asked.

---

either on the ground or under saddle, and every owner should make this clear. Rather like a child, when the horse discovers the limits of his independence he is far more stable and willing to submit.

Once in the position of having the horse's cooperation the owner can use his powers of compromise where he wishes and allow the relationship to develop from there. The horse, knowing exactly what is expected of him, will be perfectly happy with the confines of his life; he will look to his owner for direction and will not resent him for being in charge.

Hacking

Going out for a pleasant ride can give both rider and horse an ideal opportunity to get to know each other and to enjoy each other's company. Providing the horse is safe on the roads and is not going to shy at every little object it can be a relaxed occasion. The rider must realize, however, that although he hacks for his enjoyment the horse may still have hidden fears. His senses will warn him of new sights or smells, or of any strange noises, all of which may cause him to become anxious or nervous.

Traffic can be quite a problem, especially nowadays, and it is foolish to put either the horse or yourself in danger. Introducing the young animal to traffic is most important. Those who have bred their own foal will be able to let it stand with its mother near a running engine, and later beside moving vehicles, preferably on the other side of a hedge or fence. So long as the animal does not get a fright it will gradually learn not to mind bigger, more noisy vehicles.

> Horses have a remarkably strong 'homing instinct' and always know where home is. So many will drag themselves along in a disinterested way going *out* for their hack, but the minute they turn for home become wholly animated!

Other animals not previously met may cause consternation at first: sheep scuttling into the corner of a field; cows breathing through a hedge; dogs jumping at a garden gate; even a cat stealthily creeping after a mouse; all these may cause the horse to stop and stare, or even try to turn round and go home.

Going for a hack may simply be a form of entertainment for the rider and a relaxation for the horse, or it may be a method of getting the horse fit. It can even be used for teaching some exercises, such as shoulder-in or half-pass, as a change from being in the school. Whatever your purpose, it is important that when working on a hard surface such as a road, thought is given to the concussion taken by the horse's feet, legs and back in order that he is not lamed by thoughtless riding. If he is in pain he is not going to be happy or willing.

Energy

Some horses will have a great deal of natural energy, others will not. For those that do, a sensible approach should be taken, because it is useless trying to do anything with an animal with hugely pent-up energy, whether it be from temperament, over-restriction, or over-feeding. The animal must be given the opportunity to release his energy, and this is probably best done loose in an enclosed area, for safety reasons.

Unless the horse is allowed to relieve himself of his exuberance he will become increasingly agitated, perhaps developing stable vices, or even trying to rid himself of it while he is being ridden. Even placid horses need the chance to have a buck and a gallop round, but certainly the more highly strung ones will need this opportunity.

Sentiment and Fair Treatment

Many people love their horses, and I believe this should be so, but horses do suffer horribly sometimes because of it. Over-feeding is one instance: owners are anxious to give their horses as much as possible, but they allow them to become too fat so they cannot work; or they corn them up so much that they are 'out of their heads'.

There are also those well meaning but in my opinion misguided folk who 'rescue' animals from sales. Some of these have gross deformities: I saw a young animal recently whose feet had not only been neglected but one was also malformed. He could barely stand and looked utterly dejected. The owner informed me gleefully that she had saved him from the slaughterer. How terrible this was for the *horse* who would never lead a normal life.

A great many people find it difficult or impossible to have their horse 'put to sleep' when it is lame or unable to work any more. But instead of relieving their suffering, the animals are left alive, obliged to stagger about as well as they can, but often hardly able to move or dras-

tically losing condition. I knew one lady who would not have her horse put down because she could not claim the insurance! Horses are often made to work on into old age when they have lost all their agility and are riddled with arthritis.

All these owners claim to love their animals. Some horses, of course, live happily in retirement; but others who have always done a job are miserable, especially if they are suddenly given their 'freedom' – this often means they are left, alone and cold, in a field when they have been used to a pampered stable life.

Every owner must judge his own situation, and have the courage to do what is best for his animal at the end.

So-Called Habits

Most people have at some time claimed that their horse has this or that habit, whether it be an endearing one or something more unpleasant: the horse that simply will not tolerate black plastic sacks; the one that nips as you girth it up; that jumps the wheelbarrow when it is mucked out; that whinnies continuously when it is ridden; or the one that merely whickers when it hears your footsteps.

All habits have in fact evolved by discovery, accidental or otherwise, and have become in the horse's mind an entertainment, a release or pleasure. Sometimes if they become established they are very hard to break, and while we can have 'analysis' ourselves, our horse has only us to rely on.

In our dealings with him we should therefore always try to use our imagination, and to put ourselves in his place if we are really to understand what goes on in his mind.

Telepathy

When horse and owner have learned to live in harmony, each having a respect and a mutual trust, a state of almost telepathic union develops between the two. Thus in the stable the horse will move over without having to be asked, and when ridden he responds almost by thought alone; and the longer a partnership lasts and the more that the horse and rider go through together, the greater the bond between them.

As riders or owners we cannot *expect* our horse's cooperation, we must *earn* it. To have an affinity with horses is a huge advantage as instinctively we react in the right way; also the horse will differentiate and respond to those who are blessed with the sympathy and sensitivity to handle

Horses are surprisingly sensitive to disability. I have known many who have been docile, patient and willing with a very young child or a disabled rider, but who change completely with a person who is over-confident or unsympathetic!

them correctly. Thus an owner might read a hundred books or go to dozens of teachers but if it is not within his capacity to 'feel' for his horse, he will not succeed because his horse will know.

One final thought. If every owner and every rider is clever enough to leave his or her horse happy and contented at the end of each day, there is a chance that both will enjoy the following one!

Index